BOOKER PRIZE WINNERS

FOUR INDIAN NOVELISTS

Salman Rushdie • Arundhati Roy
Kiran Desai • Aravind Adiga

BOOKER PRIZE WINNERS

FOUR INDIAN NOVELISTS

Salman Rushdie • Arundhati Roy
Kiran Desai • Aravind Adiga

Edited by

R.K. Dhawan

Prestige

an international publishing house

Published by
Prestige Books
3/28, East Patel Nagar
New Delhi 110 008
Ph. 9818755529
email: prestigebooks@gmail.com
website: asiabookclub.com

Associate Office
60/29-45 Parramatta Road,
Concord, NSW 2137
Australia

ISBN: 81-7851-059-6

Printed at Chaman Offset Press, New Delhi 110 002

Contents

Kiran Desai

Aravind Adiga

Celebrating Indian Fiction

R.K. DHAWAN
University of Delhi

There are several reasons for the popularity of recent books published by Indian writers in India and abroad. Of the several qualities a book needs to have, is its capacity to capture the imagination of the reader. In other words, the most pertinent question is whether a book is 'readable.' The fiction of R.K. Narayan, Mulk Raj Anand and Anita Desai has caught the attention of the audience for one or the other reason. It may be an easy entry into the comic world, a deep concern with social problems or face to face with the dilemmas of the woman's world. At the turn of the century, however, a new trend seems to be emerging. Marketing strategies are now as important as the contents of a book or its author. Modern technology, especially the media and the Internet, has played a significant role in promoting new books. This has been quite advantageous to the third-world writers, for their books reach the world over in no time. It is no longer uncommon to see a book on the day of its release selling at different places in different countries. Books are now being treated as revenue-generating products that need, apart from other ingredients, an author who has promotion potential and a publisher with wide marketing network. This development has helped an Indian writer in English much more than a regional Indian writer. Works of new writers like Salman Rushdie, Vikram Seth, Vikram Chandra, Gita Mehta, Rohinton Mistry, Arundhati Roy, Kiran Desai and Aravind Adiga have been published by international book companies. Quality production, effective cost structure and easy mobility have given a boost to the sales: books are treated as products of a corpus culture, to be bought and sold with frenzied efforts. For example, *The Idea of India*, a diasporic book by Indian-born Oxford Professor Sunil Khilnani, has been listed by *The Guardian* among the best ten world books published in 1998.

Many of the regional writers too have been quite visible through translations. The translation phenomenon has become prominent, thanks to the efforts made by the Sahitya Akademi, Katha and other organizations. It has brought into cosmopolitan reckoning some of the brilliant writers in the regional languages. Indeed, one of the most popular novels of recent times is U.R. Anantha Murthy's *Samskara*, written originally in Kannada. The English translation by eminent poet A.K. Ramanujan may be considered a contribution both to traditional Indian literature as also to Indian English literature. The novel won the author many prestigious awards including the Sahitya Akademi and the Jnanpith Award.

India has contributed significantly to the over-all world literature. This contribution of India has been chiefly through the Indian Writing in English, novelists being in the forefront in this respect. A good number of novelists on the contemporary scene have given expression to their creative urge in no other language than English and have brought credit to the Indian English fiction as a distinctive force in the world fiction. To attempt creative expression on a national scale in an alien medium has seldom happened in human history; and it speaks of the prolific quality of the Indian mind to assimilate the newly confronting situations and the complex dilemmas of the modern world.

It is indeed amazing that as many as four Indian writers have won the prestigious Booker Award. It is heartening to learn that currently, there is a hot race for the special The Man Booker International Prize which includes two Indian writers—Mahasweta Devi and V.S. Naipaul—amongst other contenders. The £ 60,000 award, instituted in 2004, is different from the annual and better-known Man Booker Prize. This recognizes a writer's over-all contribution to the world fiction rather than judging him/ her on the basis of the current work. It is given every two years to a writer who has published fiction or whose work is generally available in translation in English. The winner will be announced in May 2009. Wishing all the best to Mahasweta Devi and V.S. Naipaul. Three cheers for Indian fiction!

V.S. Naipaul, Salman Rushdie, Arundhati Roy, Kiran Desai and Aravind Adiga as Literary Artists: A Comparative Study

S.S. GILL
Panjab University, Chandigarh

It is creditable that within a span of three decades, as many as five writers of Indian origin have received the most sought-after and coveted Booker Award for their fictional works. The present article attempts at making a comparative evaluation of these five novelists as literary artists and their contribution to the domain of Indian English fiction.

V.S. Naipaul was the first writer of Indian origin to receive the Booker Award, in the year 1971. Subsequently, he was awarded the most prestigious Nobel Prize in 2002. Naipaul is regarded a prophet, a soothsayer, a doom-watcher and a teller of unpalatable truths. When he was awarded the Bennett Award as early as 1980, he expressed his heartfelt satisfaction at the recognition accorded to his writings as a whole. He felt that it was an acceptance of the relevance of his vision and his art. Today, after he has received the Nobel Prize, he has been hailed as "the greatest living writer in the English language." He has been bracketed with as prestigious a writer as Joseph Conrad. Both these writers share a close literary kinship. Philosophically, they share a similar vision of life. It is in fact this Conradian vision which became central to Naipaul as he looked at various post-colonial societies.

In several ways, Naipaul is as enigmatic as Conrad. He eludes any specific labelling. While on the one hand, he is as serious as Conrad, on the other he is described as an excellent writer of the Comedy of Manners. He cannot be described absolutely as a social historian, a travel writer, a journalist, a biographer or a novelist. Many of the things that he gives expression to in his writings are result of his early contact with English literature when he was a student at the University of Oxford. He admits that he went to the books for 'fantasy' because, as he said, 'the English language was mine, the tradition was not.' The tradition of English and European literature was not essentially his own, for he was a third generation Indian English writer. He realized that he could write only about his society, for every writer needs a 'starting point' in order to project his fictional world. In terms of geography, he was located in a world that was far off both from West Indies as also India—the country of his heritage. Says he: 'To us, without a mythology, all literatures were foreign. Trinidad was small, remote and unimportant; and we knew we could not hope to read in books of the life we saw about us.' Since he did not have strong roots, he portrayed most authentically the anonymous man. Like Conrad's protagonists, his heroes are always in search of a more dignified life and they become acutely aware of their helplessness in achieving the goals they set for themselves. The existential question 'what is man' bothers him as much as it does Conrad.

It is primarily as a writer of diaspora and the one who gives expression to the theme of rootlessness and the crisis of identity that he is best known in the literary world. All his writings have a close relationship with his personal life. It is desirable, therefore, to have an acquaintance with V.S. Naipaul, the man. He was born in the Caribbean island of Trinidad in 1932. His grandfather had migrated from India to teach the Indian cane-workers of Trinidad. His father, Seepersad, was a journalist and a literary writer. He was a reporter in the *Trinidad Guardian* and also published a collection of short stories under the title *Gurudeva and Other Indian Tales* in 1943. His brother Shiva Naipaul was highly talented and was on his way to acquiring great popularity when he passed away in his early thirties in an accident. He published a novel entitled *Fireflies* and a collection of short stories.

Naipaul left Trinidad for England in 1950 to do English Honours at Oxford University. He graduated in 1953 and settled in England thereafter. He married Patricia Ann Hale in 1955 and decided to launch his professional career only as a writer. It was indeed a difficult resolve, for to eke out one's living by merely writing is not easy, any way. He worked as literary editor of the B.B.C. programme "Caribbean Voices" between 1954 and 1956 and reviewed constantly for the *New Statesman* between 1956 and 1960. For Naipaul, then, it was a deliberate, conscious decision to be a writer in life, despite the hazards involved in the enterprise. "I began to write," says Naipaul, "I am afraid, for no other reason than because I thought it would be nice to be a writer."

While Naipaul has produced several works, it is *A House for Mr. Biswas* that has given him name and fame. It is desirable to discuss this novel at some length. The novel deals primarily with two themes—the one being the protagonist's struggle to establish himself in a hostile environment through the ownership of a house and the other being the decline of Hindu culture under the impact of Westernization. In both these aspects, V.S. Naipaul bears close similarities to the African writer Chinua Achebe. *Things Fall Apart*, the most popular novel of Achebe, is the story of a hero who suffers a rise and fall because of his temperament and largely because of the culture-clash between the two societies, namely African and European. Like Achebe, Naipaul feels greatly concerned about the subordination of the Eastern culture to the Western. However, unlike Achebe, he is satirical and cynical in his approach. It will be important to mention here that Achebe's *Things Fall Apart* and Naipaul's *A House for Mr. Biswas* are regarded contemporary classics and, no wonder, copies of both these novels have been sold in millions.

However, it was in 1981 when Salman Rushdie's *Midnight's Children* got the Booker that Indian Writing in English came of age. Rushdie is clearly destined to be the subject of literary criticism for years to come. The novel is a Rabelaisian autobiography of Saleem Sinai whose Cyrano nose and face are compared to the map of India by his school-teacher. Salman Rushdie is an acclaimed literary figure in the modern era, and has contributed to it with eighteen novels. He is a major postcolonial writer, whose works are essentially suffused with the immigrant outlook, he being consciously aware of his Indian ancestry. He has Indian-British nationality. He takes greatly from historic allusions and religious topics in his works. He has won around 25 literary awards till date, three being the honorary Bookers (Booker Prize for *Midnight's Children* in 1981, Booker of the Bookers in 1993 and also Best of Booker for the same in 2008). He was knighted in 2007. He has been the target of active criticism for his political and religious ideas. Despite being a controversial and pretty glamorous author—with girlfriends from fashion and films—his literary prowess is unquestionable.

It was in 1997 when Arundhati Roy's novel *The God of Small Things* took the literary world by storm. Set in a small town in Kerala, it is a story of one particular family. The entire story of the novel is displayed in the very first chapter. Roy herself testifies to this: "In the first chapter I more or less tell you the story, but the novel ends in the middle of the story, and it ends with Ammu and Velutha making love and it ends on the word 'tomorrow'." The story begins with the return of Rahel to her home in Ayemenem in South India, and the reunion with her brother Estha after twenty-three years. Thus the story begins near the end of the story and is presented by a third person narrator: "It was raining when Rahel came back to Ayemenem." (1) Rahel has come back leaving her job in America, hearing that Estha is in Ayemenem again. The main event, therefore, is the presence of Rahel in the village.

The family is awaiting the arrival of Sophie Mol, the twins' half-English cousin. This forms the nucleus of the novel: the narrative moves backward and forward to the arrival and the aftermath of the death by drowning of Sophie Mol and the ill-fated love between Ammu and the untouchable Velutha. Rahel returns to Ayemenem as an adult to a decimated household, and a decaying house.

A cursory reading of the text gives the impression that the novel is quite simple, but a close study reveals that it is a well-planned work and has a subtle and complex plot. It is composed of memories treated artistically by the author. Even though the reader knows the story right at the outset, he never loses interest in the long narrative, and finds the events absorbing and interesting.

Roy's training as an architect has played a great role in building her plots. This was true in the case of the English novelist Thomas Hardy, too. Instead of practising architecture, both these writers wrote fiction and built architectonic plots. As Roy says: "the only way I wrote it was the way an architect designs a building. You know it wasn't as if I started at the beginning and ended at the end."

A characteristic feature of the novel is that it brings to life the quiet, sleepy village of Aymanam in Kerala. Roy has taken the creative writer's liberty to change the name. She spent her formative years in this village and recreates a fascinating picture of the village in her novel. Many readers find the eroticism offered by Roy's descriptions of Kerala similar to those found in a tourist book. No wonder, Ayemenem is marked in the Kerala state's latest tourist brochure. This will help in drawing the Western visitors to the state.

The next novelist to receive the Booker Award was Kiran Desai, daughter of renowned Indian writer Anita Desai, for her novel *The Inheritance of Loss* in 2006. This being her second novel, her first one *Hullabaloo in the Guava Orchard* won rave reviews and was a favourite of critics, but failed to make her a popular writer. Her second work hurled her to fame and recognition. She lived in India till the age of fourteen, then moved over to the US as permanent resident.

The Inheritance of Loss is set partly in India and partly in the U.S.A. It explores, at a deeper level, the consequences of the introduction of a western element into a non-western country, which happened during the British colonial period in India, and is happening again with India's improved relationship with America from the last decade of the 20th century.

The Inheritance of Loss is, to a large extent, a story of migration and lives being made over. In page after page, one finds the stories of Indian village life and of her people's attempts to grapple with modernity side by side with the stories of illegal immigrants in a modern centre of globalized economy and politics like New York. Both Kiran and her mother write about the Indian experience of migration. There is a common thread because the mother and the daughter have gone through the same experience.

The novel, which took eight years to complete, draws on Kiran Desai's own experience of leaving India. Even though Kiran Desai's imagination is enriched by a delectable but judicious mix of the Eastern and the Western elements, India and Indians remain at the core of her novel. The book moves back and forth from Kalimpong to Manhattan, like the author herself, and tells parallel stories of insurgency and immigration. But rediscovering her Indianness was essential to her success. Kiran, who still holds an Indian passport and feels more and more Indian, sees everything through the lens of her Indianness.

While she was writing about the immigrant experience in New York, she realized that she would have to return to India. She came back and wrote the Kalimpong bits in Kalimpong, staying in a wild and beautiful house which had been lent to her for the time. This explains why her description of both Kalimpong and Darjeeling come across as something authentic. The same is true about the political information provided in the novel.

Although the story unfolds against the background of Gorkhaland movement that rocked West Bengal for several years and irrevocably altered the political map of the Darjeeling hills, the book does not take any sides. It is equally critical about the barbarity of the state police and the inhuman violence perpetrated by the insurgents. The novel is more about the effect this movement had on the people of Kalimpong, how they reacted to it and how it changed the settled pattern of their lives than about its reasons and justification. It is about the victims and the survivors.

Kiran Desai's India is largely an imagined country. After all she had left her homeland as a school girl in her early teens. The country continues to inform and influence her literary imagination long after she has left its shores. She chose to write about the 1980s because that was the India that was most familiar to her, the place where she had lived until she was 14. But she is aware of the fact that the country she knew has changed so much so that she finds herself at a disadvantage and feels that the subject really belongs to Indian writers living in India.

In Kiran's India, people are afflicted by incurable poverty and privation. Their minds are filled with anguish and anger that result from non-fulfilment of their basic needs and that lead them to resort to terrorist violence. On the other hand, there are people who want to leave the country because of poverty, maldevelopment and lack of opportunities. But many of them find it difficult to be happy and successful in the West. The cook's son, Biju, is a representative of these Indians who live miserably both at home and abroad and whom happiness eludes forever. To people like Biju, who are enraptured by the West and blinded by the glare of American affluence, India is a backward space, an underdeveloped and uncivilized country. The backwardness of India which breeds discontent and violence, the cringing habit of her people and their willingness 'to undergo any kind of humiliation to get into the States' (184)—all these are, her detractors believe, facets of a myth which diasporic writers like Kiran Desai, with their eyes on the Western readers, seek to perpetrate. They seem to forget conveniently, or—to be more precise, try to ignore, the 'other' India which exists outside this marketable myth. The story of the 'other,' self-reliant, and self-respecting India is not received cordially in the West, because the sale value of that story is minimal. To write in English is to write for the non-Indians, to write for their satisfaction, to sustain and reinforce their beliefs, to translate India and Indianness, according to their predilections. Kiran's novel bears ample testimony to this unavoidable literary phenomenon.

The writer, who recently received the Booker Prize, is Aravind Adiga for his rather controversial novel *The White Tiger*. Aravind Adiga was born in Madras in 1974 and has subsequently lived in India, Australia, the U.S. and the U.K. He currently lives in Mumbai. *The White Tiger* is his first novel.

The novel sketches the life and character of one Balram Halwai, who immediately catches our imagination. It is a tale of two Indias. Balram's journey from the darkness of village life to the light of entrepreneurial success is utterly amoral, brilliantly irreverent, deeply endearing and altogether unforgettable.

Born in a village in the dark heart of India, the son of a rickshaw-puller, Balram is taken out of school by his family and put to work in a teashop. As he crushes coal and wipes tables, he nurses a dream of escape—of breaking away from the banks of Mother Ganga into whose murky depths have seeped the remains of a hundred generations.

His big chance comes when a rich village landlord hires him as a chauffeur for his son, daughter-in-law and their two Pomeranian dogs. From behind the wheel of a Honda, Balram first sees Delhi. The city is a revelation. Amid the cockroaches and call-centres, the 36,000,004 gods, the slums, the shopping malls and the crippling traffic jams, Balram's re-education begins. Caught between his instinct to be a loyal son and servant, and his desire to better himself, he learns of a new morality at the heart of a new India. As the other servants flick through the pages of Murder Weekly, Balram begins to see how the Tiger might escape his cage. For surely any successful man must spill a little blood on his way to the top.

The narrator, Balram Halwai, portrays within a period of seven nights the pangs of post-Raj Indian democratic set-up. Being a chauffeur to a landlord from his village, Balram writes letters (not to be posted) to the premier of China, Wen Jiabao, picturing an authentic portrait of the modern Independent India. Adiga does not fear "attacks at home for his portrayal of India. . .

'The greatest-living India painter M.F. Hussain lives in exile'. I'm in a different position from Hussain . . . the political class does not read. He lives in exile because his messages got through, but mine probably won't." *The White Tiger* is presented in the form of epistolary novel in which, the protagonist Balram, narrates his rags-to-riches story to the premier of China, Wen Jiabao, who is to visit Bangalore, India's Information Technology capital. The narrator gives all details to the visiting leader as that "he wouldn't be fooled by any of the false pictures to politicians he meets might paint about life in India when he comes for his official state visit." At the outset, Balram tells his own story of life.

Halwai has come from 'the heart of rural India'; he manages to escape his family and poverty by becoming chauffeur to a landlord from his village. He often goes to Delhi with this landlord to bribe government officials. He drives him around the capital as he greases the palms of all the various political 'fixers' and parliamentarians that need greasing in order to ensure the family business survives. Balram narrates that in his small village everybody is beholden to one of the four landlords. "If you want to grow anything you have to pay money to one person. If you want to graze animals you have to pay money to another. If you want to use the roads to make money as a rickshaw driver, you pay 10% of everything you earn to a third. Finally, the fourth one owns the waters. If you want to fish or use the water to transport goods, you pay him."

Balram tells that his family is forced to borrow money from one of the landlords to pay for his cousin's dowry. He has to leave school and start working in tea houses. Balram is destined for greater things. His grandmother comes up with six hundred rupees so he might learn to drive and get a job driving for a wealthy man. Through blind luck he happens to show up at his landlord's compound on the day the youngest son has returned from America and needs his own driver. Thus begins his long climb out of the darkness of poverty.

Balram tells how he becomes a successful entrepreneur and his journey from a small non-descript village Laxmangarh to Bangalore. Within this story is contained this perspective of the one who exits on the periphery and his response to each and every situation that he encounters in modern India. Born to a rickshaw-puller, living in the small village of Laxmangarh, the protagonist does not even have a name that he can call his own and is named Balram by his teacher the day he is sent to school. "It is a village that represents at least a third of the country, a fertile place, full of rice fields and wheat fields and ponds."[4] But those who live in this village call it the 'Darkness'. Adiga makes it vividly clear at the outset of the novel, "that India is two countries in one: an India of light and an India of darkness (14). Balram is extraordinarily responsive to the world around him, and through his observations the reader gets to know the two Indias. While Balram's village is the model of all the amenities that are provided by the government in its plans, reality is that everything in the village is defunct and broken. Its people are malnourished and lead a life of utter misery and poverty, leading a day-to-day existence without any hope for a better future. Balram slowly manages to distance himself from his family and gets a job with Mr. Ashok and his wife Pinky. This job opens up new avenues for his inquisitive mind, and here the reader is informed in great details about the haves and have-nots in India, and the manner in which the people employed as domestic help are treated. Balram keeps his eyes and ears open for any information. It takes no time to realize that hierarchy and corruption are the rule of the day.

Balram is not jut a driver. It turns out he is expected to cook, clean and do whatever else his master needs him to do. As the novel progresses, Balram becomes a witness to the glitz as well as the unjust system around him and begins to question his position as a servant, his place in society which leads to his resenting his conditioning for such a life. He begins to long for a better life for himself and is no longer proud to wear the driver's uniform, which in the beginning of the novel had so fascinated him. He wants to wear good clean clothes, go to places his master and mistress visit and in short he begins desiring the basic things of life which have so far been denied to him by circumstances.

Amongst the writers discussed as literary artists, the most talked about writer in English-speaking world today is Salman Rushdie, who mainly thrives on the controversial content of his fictional world. But the true successor to the legacy of Charles Dickens, perhaps the greatest English novelist of all times, is V.S. Naipaul who for nearly fifty years has been entertaining his readers all over the world with a mixed bag of writing that combines fiction, autobiography and travelogue. Arundhati Roy is the writer of the mega wonder novel *The God of Small Things* who depicts the socio-political milieu of Kerala during the Sixties. Kiran Desai in her novel The Inheritance of Loss takes us to the exotic world, that is India. And lastly, Aravind Adiga in The White Tiger offers a graphic picture of contemporary India, in a most dexterous fashion.

Bibliography

Adiga, Aravind. *Between the Assassinations* (Picador 2008).
_____. *The White Tiger*. Harper Collins: New Delhi, 2008.
Desai, Kiran. *The Inheritance of Loss*. Penguin, 2006.
Marcus, Richard. *The White Tiger*, Book Review (May 2, 2008).
Roy, Arundhati. *The God of Small Things*. New Delhi: IndiaInk, 1997.
Rushdie, Salman. *Midnight's Children*. London: Picador, 1981.

Salman Rushdie's *Midnight's Children*: A Critical Study

TAPAN KUMAR GHOSH
University of Burdwan

Salman Rushdie shot into international fame with the publication of his second novel, *Midnight's Children*,[1] in 1980. The book won the prestigious Booker McConnell Prize for fiction in 1981 and was hailed as a literary masterpiece. The award gave it enormous publicity and media coverage, unlocking a flood of reviews and articles, radio-features and interviews. The novel was received, both in India and abroad, with enthusiastic and almost unanimous acclaim. Sceptical voices were silenced by exuberant rhetoric and hymnic panegyrics. Rushdie was accepted as a major writer and ranked with such widely diverse authors as Henry Fielding, Laurence Sterne, Rabelais, Charles Dickens, Franz Kafka, James Joyce, Gabriel Garcia Marquez, Gunter Grass and Milan Kundera. The book rode a wave of popularity unprecedented in the history of Indian writing in English.

More than twenty years have passed after that sensational event. Rushdie has published five more novels in the intervening period. One of them shook the world as no book had done before. But *Midnight's Children*, unlike many award-winning novels, continues to be read and discussed with interest not only by ordinary readers but by literary critics as well. The passage of time has sobered the uncritical enthusiasm and created a space for balanced critical judgement. The socio-economic and literary changes which have taken place both in and outside India and the tumultuous events of Rushdie's own life—particularly the controversy over *The Satanic Verses*—have made critics and scholars more guarded in their response to *Midnight's Children* and its author. Initially described as a comic-epic in prose about the picaresque journey of a fabulous hero whose birth coincided with India's Independence and whose life encapsulates the experience of the country, the novel has gradually been subsumed in a theoretical discourse on nation, nationalism and postcoloniality. It is now regarded as a foundational text of postcolonial novel which challenges the authority of imperial textuality and disrupts the cultural and linguistic stability of the colonizing centre. It shows an alternative way of conceiving history that breaks down barriers between cultures. Others have viewed the book as a fictional representation of the postmodernist celebration of fragmentation, multiplicity and self-reflexivity. Rushdie's perception that all narratives are susceptible to being re-written, his insistence on the 'provisional nature of all truths' and his narrativization of 'slices' in the form of 'fragments of broken mirrors'[2] also refurbish his disposition towards postmodernism. Critics have written about his multiple literary influences, his fusion of Indian oral tradition and Western novel genre, and his innovative use of language. Everybody in India was not, however, amused by the book's commercial success. Some severely criticized its 'chutnification' of Indian history while others challenged Rushdie's claim for radical innovations in language and style. It was argued that Rushdie could not be considered as an Indian author because of his outsider position and that the success of *Midnight's Children* was largely due to international publicity. But few people now deny its influence on younger writers for whom the book released a new spring of creativity and heralded a spirit of freedom. A whole generation of young, and largely male, authors (Amitav Ghosh, Allan Sealy, Shashi Tharoor, Mukul Kesavan, Rohinton Mistry, Vikram Seth, Vikram Chandra—to name only a few) followed in his footsteps. They were infected by Rushdie's confident use of English and inspired by his acknowledgement of multiple viewpoints and narrative modes as well as his audacious attempt to place the marginalized story of an individual or a family at the centerstage of national drama. *Midnight's Children* has been recognized as a landmark novel, an important turning point in post-Independence Indian fiction in English. Its runaway success catalysed a spectacular resurgence of Indian English novel and brought about a remarkable change in the attitude of the reading public in India and abroad towards this phenomenon which had remained, until then, a largely walled-in literary entity.

Publicity and literary awards (the Booker, and subsequently the Booker of Bookers, the James Tait Black Memorial Book Prize and the American English Speaking Union Literary Award) no doubt contributed to the popularity of *Midnight's Children*. But the time was also most opportune for a dramatic change. Indian English novel had reached a stagnant stage, in terms of both content and form, by the end of the nineteen seventies. The old masters of the craft like Mulk Raj Anand, Raja Rao and R.K. Narayan, who had started writing in the 1930s, reached their peak by the 1960s. No new novelist drew the attention of serious readers after Arun Joshi and Anita Desai. Experimentation with either language or form was conspicuous by its absence. The readers were tired of the realistic portrayal of social ills, East-West cultural encounters, and individual's alienation from society and self which had been catered to them with unflagging regularity since Independence. At the end of the decade, Indian English novel reached an impasse and required a radical reformulation. The comet-like arrival of *Midnight's Children* with a stupendous aesthetic force galvanized the sluggish literary scene by reconceptualizing the novel—its form, content and narrative mode—and re-inventing its medium. It infused new life into Indian English novel and set the trend for a whole generation of writers. It broke the ground rules of the older form of fiction and created new rules without any apology or explanation, foreword or footnote. It broke away not only from the earlier tradition of Indian English novel but also from the Western depictions of India as one finds in the works of Paul Scott, E.M. Forster and V.S. Naipaul. Its thematic and stylistic concerns called for a new experimental strategy which is mirrored in its mode of narration, complex mixture of different narrative genres, novelty of metaphors and inventiveness of idiom. The novel brings together public and private events, history, myth and legends, realism and fantasy, hilarious comedy and scathing satire—within an imaginative and linguistic framework which is always under control. It flamboyantly crosses, fragments and parodies different narrative styles and perspectives, adopts—often subverts—Western genres and employs traditional local forms in a contemporary context to serve 'a huge purpose, namely the personification of India and the realization of Indian life'[3] with all its contradictions and its polyphonic plurality and cultural multiplicity.

Anyone reading Rushdie's works is struck by his obvious attachment to his Indian roots. His education and his adult life have been British. But a strong part of him still identifies with India and his imagination continues to feed on the sub-continent. His works carry a deep imprint of the complex socio-cultural scene of India which has a significant bearing on the thematic as well as stylistic aspect of his fiction. It is this as well as his passionate involvement with the history and politics of his country which has induced many critics to consider him as an Indian writer in English. But in reality his novels provide a curious mix of Eastern and Western elements. Rushdie is a product of biculturalism which is regarded by many as the 'creative matrix' of his fiction. He is at home in the East and the West and the two diametrically opposite cultures have defined his identity and his writing. His split identity leads him to search for his literary ancestry in both the cultures (just as Saleem Sinai's obsession with the tracing of ancestry in *Midnight's Children* is an attempt to come to terms with his divided identity.) His novels have come to be viewed as a new kind of postcolonial writing in which a migrant, diasporic and cosmopolitan consciousness dominates. They are hybrid, multi-lingual and conversant with the cultural codes of the West, at the same time retaining their thematic connections with the country of his origin. This paradoxical dual position, as insider and outsider in the society he writes about, informs and animates his writing even today. Rushdie has discussed this problematic question of identity in several essays and interviews. He is not worried about the negative connotations associated with such a position and about criticism, both in India and in the West, that his works lack authenticity and are informed by political cynicism and lack of commitment, his hybridity being primarily an aesthetic device, a source of themes. He has stressed that assimilating Western and Oriental literary traditions should not be regarded as disloyalty towards one's cultural heritage but as a bridging of gaps. Rushdie has reiterated that for postcolonial migrant writers like him, who inhabit a fractured, hybrid world and are multi-lingual by necessity, the experience of cultural translation (he has called himself a 'translated man' and labelled postcolonial migrant literature in English as poly-cultural 'translated writing') is an aesthetic bliss. It not only supplies material for their works but also gives a valuable insight on the conditions of their home countries. The experience of 'straddling cultures' (*IH*, 15) provides the migrant writers with double perspective or, to use a metaphor from *Midnight's Children*, a 'stereo-scopic vision' on their dislocated world. A hybrid postcolonial text, *Midnight's Children* achieves a successful, and aesthetically satisfying, fusion of East and West in terms of both form and content. This hybridity or cultural mix, which is intrinsic to all of Rushdie's works and explains much of his versatility, has been valorized by postcolonial critical theory.

Midnight's Children had its genesis in a family joke: two months after Rushdie was born, the British ran away from India! As he recalls:

> This joke was always told to embarrass me at awkward moments, which gave me the idea to take a child and a country, and to join them comically. From that there was a short step to having the idea of a child that was born exactly at the moment of independence, and who believed himself to be connected to the country. Then, there was the story of the child growing up and the country growing up, so to say, in parallel, it began with that.[4]

This provides the central thesis of the novel, that the life of a midnight's child born on 15 August 1947 is analogous to that of the emerging history of the nation born at the same moment, and that the telling of the thirty-year-old story of the protagonist is the same as narrating the postcolonial history of the country. It allows Rushdie to relate private life and public events and examine the relationship between individual and history. By locking together the destinies of the man and the nation, he makes his narrator-protagonist, Saleem Sinai, a witness to the evolving history of the nation.

One way of connecting the individual member of society with the collective stream of history is writing history as autobiography. The very opening paragraph of *Midnight's Children* establishes Rushdie's narrative method, his interplay of history ('India's arrival at Independence'), autobiography ('I was born in the city of Bombay') and fantasy ('once upon a time'). This interplay is sustained throughout the narrative which has a tripartite structure, consisting of three books and thirty chapters which roughly correspond to the thirty years of Saleem's life and India's thirty-year course from Independence to Emergency. History provides the book with its narrative axis and the linearity of public events holds the novel together. All the important historical events in the sub-continent, from the Jallianwala Bagh massacre (1919) to the Emergency (1975) are ingeniously linked with the crucial turns in the story of Saleem and his family so that the autobiography of an individual reads like the history of a country and the odyssey of a family becomes the odyssey of a nation from 1915 to 1977, the period of Indian history Rushdie charts in the novel.

In his quest for individual identity, Saleem ventures to rewrite the entire history of his times from random shards of memory, all the while conscious of falling victim 'to the temptation of every autobiographer that since the past exists only in one's memories . . . it is possible to create past events simply by saying they occurred.' (443) He makes no distinction between official facts and gossips, history and legends because he believes that sometimes 'legends make reality, and become more useful than the facts.' (47) He takes liberty with chronology and blends history with fiction, allowing concocted stories to encroach upon recorded events, in order to preserve the correspondence between his life and the history of India and create the illusion of himself as a protagonist at the centre. Saleem knows that he cannot lay claim to objectivity and that the reconstitution of his history is bound to be largely fictive because of his egotistical and selective framework of reference, his fallible memory which constantly plays tricks and provides an excuse for factual errors and unreliability, and his partial, fragmentary vision represented by his mnemonic icon, the perforated sheet. Despite his intention to produce a comprehensive account of the past with its continuities and missing links, he is condemned by his heritage—his grandfather's perforated sheet—'to see [his] own life—its meanings, its structures—in fragments.' (107) Implicit in his statement is the admission that human beings are 'capable only of fractured perceptions,' (*IH*, 12) and that all reclamations of the past are bound to be provisional and incomplete. He attempts to re-imagine the past and restore it to himself with the aid of memory. What his narrative presents is not literal truth but 'memory's truth' which 'selects, eliminates, alters, exaggerates, minimizes, glorifies, and vilifies also; but in the end it creates its own reality, its heterogeneous but usually coherent version of events.' (211) Rushdie foregrounds memory as an inextricable aspect of his delineation of India and makes the subject of the novel 'the way we remake the past to suit our present purposes, using memory as our tool.' (*IH*, 10) *Midnight's Children* is an affirmation of the importance of memory in the reclamation of personal and collective history and the constitution of the individual's identity. Saleem compares his presentation of history through memory to the pickling process ('chutnification') which invariably leads to alteration and transformation: 'in words and pickles, I have immortalized my memories, although distortions are inevitable in both methods.' (459) The pickle metaphor suggests that history, reshaped ('chutnified') through the imagination of a creative artist, becomes a kind of fiction. Saleem's story is not authentic history; it only plays with historical shapes. *Midnight's Children* offers a fictional alternative to the official history of the country. As Rushdie says: "what I was actually doing was a novel of memory and about memory, so that my India was just that: 'my' India, a version and no more than one version of all the hundreds of millions of possible versions." (*IH*, 10) He presents the postcolonial history of India from the point of view of an individual. Rushdie seems to suggest that individual reclamation of the past provides a version of truth which is valid for the individual.

Saleem essays a revisionist history which destabilizes the certainty of the official version and offers a critique of authority. For example, the state truth of Pakistan about the Bangladesh War in 1971 and the official view of the Emergency—that no atrocities were committed by the Pakistani army in the East Wing and that there were no excesses like forced sterilization and slum clearance during the period of Indira Gandhi's authoritarian rule—are given the lie in Saleem's remembered version of the events. Rushdie believes that both writers and politicians 'try to make the world in their own images; they fight for the same territory.' (*IH*, 14) He uses the 'novel of memory' as a political weapon to disprove the politicians' version of truth and resist the forgetfulness which is induced by their distortion, even alteration, of history. In the first section of the novel that describes India's colonial past, Saleem's narrative debunks the myths which sustained the Empire ('Methwold') and shatters the idols of imperial history. A paradigmatic postcolonial text, *Midnight's Children* challenges the ideologically determined patterns of historical relationships. In this book, the natives of India do not play only side-roles or bit-parts in British history, as in the novels of M.M. Kaye and Paul Scott; they rather make history. It seeks to emancipate the formerly colonized people from the reverential awe in which they held the colonizers. The imposing figure of Mountbatten is reduced to insignificance ('Mountbatten with his extraordinary haste and his chicken-breast eater of a wife') and

General Dyer is remembered only as a tyrant devoid of human emotions ('Mercurochrome'). The British transfer of power is parodied through the symbolic takeover of the intact Englishness of the Methwold's Estate. Rushdie ruthlessly attacks British colonialism through his caricature of characters like Methwold and attempts to link many of the ills which plague independent India to the mischief done by the British during their rule. What was invisible or forcibly silenced in the British history (like the story of the nationalist Muslims in 'Hit-the-Spittoon' and 'Under the Carpet') is brought to focus through an effective blend of fact and fiction. Saleem's oral narrative supplants the recorded British history of colonized India with a counter discourse that subverts and undermines the colonizers' view of the country. Rushdie's fabulism—his fusion of fact and fantasy—also contributes to this alternative version of history. Historical events, when viewed through the fractured lenses of a fallible memory and connected with myths and legends, lose their unidimensional veracity and appear fantastic. *Midnight's Children*, a novel about the textuality of history, replaces the unitary narrative of official history of India with a comprehensive and highly subjective version of the multi-dimensional reality of the sub-continent. It reads like a spoof on the traditional histories of the country which are no more than biographies of viceroys and generals, Presidents and Prime Ministers, and suggests that the autobiography of an ordinary individual can participate in, and significantly contribute to, the making of national history.

What gives *Midnight's Children*—which is chiefly about India, the country of Rushdie's own cherished childhood—its narrative breadth is the connection with autobiography. There is a close connection between the writer Salman and the narrator-protagonist Saleem. Rushdie himself acknowledges this identity: 'The fact that he is called Saleem and I am called Salman . . . it's not surprising that the identification is made.'[5] The narrative voice is put in Saleem's mouth and the first person narration lends the work an immense intensity. There is a lot of autobiographical material in the novel but it is sifted to suit the story's requirement. Rushdie's family, like Saleem's, hailed from Kashmir. His maternal grandfather was a doctor attached to the Aligarh University in U.P. As in the novel, the Partition split Rushdie's family. His parents migrated to Pakistan in 1964. Both the writer and his hero were born in 1947, within eight weeks of each other, and had an Anglicized upbringing in Bombay, a city nostalgically evoked in the novel. *Midnight's Children* is, like *The Moor's Last Sigh*, essentially a Bombay novel. Almost half the book takes place in this city. Rushdie has admitted in several interviews that he had always desired to write a long novel about Bombay of the 1950s and early 1960s. The cosmopolitan city with its composite culture and linguistic plurality becomes for him a metaphor of the multiplicity of urban India. The spirit of Bombay, both as a place and as an idea, permeates the book. Bombay cinema, the city's biggest cultural production and the most ubiquitous icon of India's popular culture, forms an important inter-text of *Midnight's Children*. This intertextuality is evident in the adoption of filmic terminology into the narrative. 'Nobody from Bombay should be without a basic film vocabulary' (33), says Saleem who has an insider's knowledge of the conventions of Hindi cinema. He uses this knowledge not only to construct his narrative but also to colour and interpret it for the readers. The novel simulates, and often parodies, the Bombay films' fantastic and melodramatic mode, incorporating formulaic devices like mistaken identities, changes of babies at birth, doubles, multiple parents, amnesia and accidental return of memory, and movie-trailers or previews involving anticipatory mention of events to come. The metaphor of a cinema screen is employed to discuss the question of perspective (165-66) while a film cliché—'a calendar ruffled by a breeze, its pages flying off in rapid succession' (346)—solves the problem of describing the passage of time. Saleem uses close-ups and long-shots to situate the reader in relation to the action. Dreams and fantasies, myths and legends—the stock-in-trade of Bombay cinema—are persistently used in the novel. Rushdie believes, very much like the Latin American magic realists, that the unreal and the bizarre are often a more accurate mirror of truth and that only the epic-fabulist mode can faithfully reflect the fantastic complexities of a vast country like India. Uncle Hanif succeeded as a film-maker when he adopted this unrealistic mode in 'Lovers of Kashmir.' But his naturalistic film about an ordinary pickle factory and its humble labourers flopped because, as Saleem says, 'in the temple of illusions, he had become the high priest of reality.' (244) Thus, in *Midnight's Children*, melodrama piles upon melodrama as Saleem's life acquires 'the colouring of a Bombay talkie.' (148)

Saleem sets out to write his autobiography near the end of his battered life in the hope that his mnemonic enterprise may achieve the significance which the events of his adulthood have drained from him. The act of recollection and recording becomes a sort of cathartic attempt to resist his fragmentation and regain control ('I must retain control as long as possible' [461]). His greatest desire is for meaning, and making sense of his marginalized life takes on the dimension of a life and death struggle: 'I must work fast, faster than Scheherazade, if I am to end up meaning—yes, meaning—something. I admit it: above all things, I fear absurdity.' (9) *Midnight's Children* begins and ends with explicit references to *A Thousand and One Nights* which provides Saleem with the organizing principle of his narrative—preservation and justification of life by story-telling. Like the imperilled Princess, Saleem tells his story, which is also the history of his time and place, within a framed narrative to a clearly defined listener (Padma) who functions as an implied reader within the text and as a continuous reminder of the present tense of the narrating time.

The narrative begins with an announcement of Saleem's portentous birth 'at the precise instant of India's arrival at independence.' (9) In order to account for it, he takes the readers back, with the help of his 'all-knowing memory,' (88) to his origin, his grandfather—the progressive doctor Aadam Aziz. Book One, consisting of eight chapters, traces the family's journey from Kashmir via Agra and Delhi to Bombay which becomes, synecdochally, the march of the country from colonial rule to Independence. All the major historical events from 1915 to 1947 are meticulously interlaced with Saleem's family saga: the Jallianwala Bagh tragedy, Muslim League and its communal politics, the role of the nationalist Muslims who opposed the idea of Pakistan, 'Quit India' movement, Cabinet Mission and its failure, the arrival of Mountbatten, the partition of the country and the consequent riots and bloodshed. Saleem's nativity marks the dividing line between the old world and the new. The dream of the nation born at the numinous midnight of August 15 amidst Nehru's legendary narration of postcoloniality in the Assembly Hall is embodied by the one thousand and one magical children. Born with miraculous powers between midnight and 1 a.m., they represent the unbounded optimism and marvellous promises of the nascent state. Saleem's autobiography is, in fact, the story of these children who are privileged to be both masters and victims of their time: 'The children of midnight were also the children of the time: fathered . . . by history.' (118) A sort of multi-headed monster, speaking in the myriad tongues of Babel, the midnight's children are a metaphor of heterogeneous Indian society, its very essence of multiplicity. Saleem is the spokesman of these children whom he unites in the parliament of his mind. By virtue of his synchronous birth with the nation at the exact stroke of midnight, Saleem claims 'a place at the centre of the things' (238) and feels responsible for the country's fate to which he is 'indissolubly chained.' (9) He is literally 'handcuffed to history,' (9) the circumstances of his birth making him analogous to the newly independent nation of India. His narrative is thus both a story of his own life and a mirror of the nation. Prime Minister Nehru's letter celebrating the illustrious moment of Saleem's birth identifies his life with the life of India itself and confers on him the 'role of the mirror of the nation.' (427) Book Two charts the dynamic growth of Saleem from childhood to adolescence which reflects the development of free India between 1947 and 1965. All the national and sub-continental events of consequence during this period of the country's postcolonial history are linked with Saleem's career: the assassination of Mahatma Gandhi, India's Five Year Plans, reorganization of Indian states and language riots, the imposition of Martial Law in Pakistan, the Chinese aggression, the theft of the holy relic in Srinagar's Hazratbal mosque, Nehru's death and the Indo-Pakistani War of 1965. At the autobiographical level, this section traces the ups and downs in the fortunes of Sinai family, the birth of Saleem's sister, the disintegration of Midnight Children's Conference, the death of Aadam Aziz and uncle Hanif, and the revelation of Mary Pereira's crime which exposes Saleem as an imposter and shatters his dream world. The Sinais migrate to Pakistan where Saleem reaches a tumultuous adulthood and witnesses the annihilation of his family in the war of 1965. Saleem's narration of the evolution of India since Independence is punctuated with many scandalous events which shook the nation while his treatment of the history of Pakistan is peppered with episodes of political grotesquerie. The ungainly shape that Independence took in the subcontinent and the deplorable developments of the twin nations which made Saleem and his family helpless victims meet with a severe indictment in his narrative. Rushdie noticed a downward slide in post-Independence India, particularly after the demise of Nehru. The euphoria of Independence lasted upto the first decade and then gradually gave way to despair. Progress of the country yielded to fanaticism and stunted growth and the body politic, like Saleem's fissured body, began to crack. With the decay of the myth of the nation, Saleem's sense of engagement was replaced by doubt, cynicism and withdrawal. Book Three deals with the Bangladesh war of 1971, the Emergency and its aftermath. This is a darker and more political section than the other two. The narrative in this part becomes less digressive and the political satire more devastating. Saleem, with his dream of saving the nation from her fate, is drawn into the vortex of politics which crushes him and leaves him impotent and marginalized. Rushdie is highly critical of Indira Gandhi's authoritarian rule between 1975 and 1977 (metaphorically described as an 'endlessly prolonged midnight' [419]) because it irreparably damaged Indian reality and betrayed the country's secular-democratic ideals.[6] The hopes of the nation generated at the moment of Independence were drained with the castration of the midnight's children by Indira Gandhi, called the 'Black Widow,' and her sinister minions. Disillusioned and impotent, Saleem retires to the privacy of a pickle factory and decides to preserve ('chutnify') his version of India's history for future generation before his demise. Saleem's progress from unlimited optimism to disenchantment, from illusion of centrality to marginalization and impotence, which parallels the journey of independent India from an optimistic and vibrant nation to a despairing and comatose state, is a telling comment on the postcolonial history of the country. The title *Midnight's Children*, drawn from the hour of India's Independence on 15 August, 1947, suggests both the promise of a new future that the one thousand and one children symbolized and the failure of the post-Independence generation to fulfil that promise and realize their potential to build 'the noble mansion of free India, where all her children may dwell,' (118) as Nehru had famously said in his speech at that momentous hour. The freedom's children betrayed the idea of a unified and secular India with their confusion, internal rivalry, divisiveness and parochialism. Their story is, in fact, about these 'broken promises; made to be broken.' (439) Rushdie himself admitted in an interview (1985) that if the novel had any purpose, it was to "say that the thirty-two years between independence and the end of the book didn't add up to very much, that a kind of betrayal had taken place, and that the book was dealing with the nature of that betrayal."

Midnight's Children has been criticized in India for its despairing tone. It has been alleged that the book's description of India is pessimistic. Rushdie, however, repudiates the charge of pessimism, claiming that the novel's structure itself indicates a forward-looking attitude. The ending of Saleem's narrative is no doubt bleak suggesting the defeat of the human spirit but, Rushdie thinks, the last pages of the book hint at the emergence of a newer, tougher and more pragmatic generation (represented by Saleem's strong-willed son Aadam Sinai) who takes over from the children of midnight. Distancing himself from the point of view of the narrator-protagonist, he says:

> What I tried to do was to set up a tension in the text, a paradoxical opposition between the form and content of the narrative. The story of Saleem does indeed lead him to despair. But the story is told in a manner designed to echo . . . the Indian talent for non-stop self-regeneration. That is why the narrative throws up new stories, why it 'teems.' (*IH*, 16)

The novel's multitudinous form, suggesting the inexhaustible possibilities of the country for rejuvenation, thus, counterbalances Saleem's personal tragedy and its textual plenitude offsets his dismal view of India's political impoverishment and historical grotesquerie.

NOTES

1. Salman Rushdie, *Imaginary Homelands*: *Essays and Criticism* 1981-1991 (London: Granta, 1991), pp. 10-12.
2. William Walsh, "India and the Novel," *The New Pelican Guide to English Literature*, ed. Boris Ford (Penguin, 1983), p. 257.
3. Salman Rushdie, *Midnight's Children* (London: Picador, 1981), p. 308.
4. M.L. Pandit, 'An Interview with Salman Rushdie,' *New Commonwealth Writing* (New Delhi: Prestige, 1996), p. 44.
5. Rani Dharkar, 'An Interview with Salman Rushdie,' *New Quest*, 42 (November-December 1983), p. 351.
6. Rushdie's views on the excesses of Emergency are depressing. He represents Indira's unmitigated villainy in misogynistic terms. No wonder that *Midnight's Children* provoked the anger of Nehru's daughter who brought and won a libel suit against the author. Some offending remarks were expunged from the novel.

History as a Mode of Literature: A Study of *Midnight's Children*

REENA MITRA
Christ Church College, Kanpur

In *Midnight's Children*, Salman Rushdie makes Indian history a co-ordinate in his fictional art—his presentation of historical facts covers a vast span, from the pro-Independence Jalianwala Bagh incident of 1919 to the period of Emergency in 1977, and adopts a variant mode of portrayal. The facts themselves are of little interest as they have been repeatedly given to us by several novelists as well as historians. What is significant is how Rushdie has fantasized his depiction of historical reality. The introduction of the element of the magical and the supernatural has lent the work a dimension that makes it characteristically Rushdie's own, for he has his typical way of concocting a blend of art and life.

"Art," as Kakutani observes, "does have a way of imitating life and writers have always been skeptical or incapable of unilaterally separating the two."[1] Salman Rushdie, too, in writing *Midnight's Children*, seems unable, by nature and by intention, to dissever the two. He had started, as Zola believed every literary artist did, "from the true facts, which are our indestructible basis, but to show "the mechanism of these facts,"[2] he had to modify them and it is in this specific orientation given to facts that his distinctive genius lies. By his own admission it is in *Midnight's Children* that he finds his "true voice."[3]

Nancy E. Batty, in her comparative study of the narrative techniques of *Midnight's Children* and *A Thousand and One Nights*[4] draws careful attention to the dramatization of "the problematical relationship of life to art, art to life"[5] in *Midnight's Children*. This dramatization, she argues, is the effect of the deliberate juxtaposition of "the oriental tale, the eighteenth century Shandean novel and the modern historical 'realities' of India."[6]

In an article in defence of his novel, *The Satanic Verses*, Rushdie has made his aesthetic predilections very clear when he says: "do not ask your writers to create 'typical' or 'representative' fictions. Such books are almost invariably dead books."[7] The novels that he really cares for are "those which attempt radical reformulation of language, form and ideas, those that attempt to do what the 'novel' seems to insist upon: to see the world new."[8] And, this novel worldview, if it provides implications that are worth thinking about, fulfils one of the important functions of literature.

Midnight's Children is a literary response to a series of real life situations that have been cleverly fictionalized through allusions disguised as well as direct, to the country's recent as well as not so recent past. The novel has an epic sweep[9] covering about six decades in the history of the Indian subcontinent. Book One covers the time from the Jallianwala Bagh incident in April 1919 to the birth of the protagonist, Saleem, on August 15,1947; Book Two extends upto the end of the Indo-Pakistan war in September 1965, and Book Three envelops the period upto the end of the Emergency in March, 1977, and includes the Bangladesh war as well.

At the fictional level, *Midnight's Children* depicts the events and experiences in the lives of three generations of the Sinai family. The account begins with their days in Srinagar and follows their passage through Amritsar, Agra and Bombay to Karachi from where Saleem alone returns hidden in the basket of Parvati, the witch,[10] only to experience the tremors of the Emergency that had been clamped in India. At the semantic level, it is far more complex and has intriguing social and political connotations.

A careful analysis of *Midnight's Children* reveals three major aspects of Rushdie's use of history in his novel that deserve study: (i) the commingling of autobiography and narrative, (ii) the striking breach of chronology and (iii) the search for identity and the meaning of life. The opening page of the novel gives us a decipherable clue to them. Characteristically, Rushdie begins:

> I was born in the city of Bombay. . . . once upon a time. No, that won't do there's no getting away from the date: I was born in Dr. Narlikar's Nursing Home on August 15, 1947. And the time? . . . On the stroke of midnight, as a matter of fact . . . at the precise instant of India's arrival at independence, I tumbled forth into the world. . . . I had been mysteriously handcuffed to history, my destinies indissolubly chained to those of my country. For the next three decades, there was to be no escape. . . . I, Saleem Sinai, . . . had become heavily embroiled in Fate—at the best of times, a dangerous sort of involvement.
>
> Now, however, time (having no further use for me) is running out. I will soon be thirty-one years old. . . . I must work fast . . . if I am to end up meaning—yes, meaning—something.
>
> And there are so many stories to tell, too many, such an excess of intertwined lives events miracles places rumours, so dense a commingling of the improbable and the mundane! I must commence the business of remaking my life from the point at which it really began, some thirty-two years before anything as obvious, as present, as my clock-ridden, crime-stained birth. [11] (1-2)

The very first sentence of the work is illustrative of the hybrid art of the novelist. The tale is meant to be at once an autobiography and a narrative, an account of facts and a yarn spun out of imagination, a blend of truth and fiction. "I was born in the city of Bombay" clearly sets the tone for an autobiography but the latter half of the sentence shifts the reader's attention and focus, and leaves him baffled as he makes a futile attempt to approximate fiction while facts call for their share of attention. He is mystified as to how "once upon a time" can be a natural sequel to what goes before. And yet, the two are confidently set against each other as a revelatory beginning to "so dense a commingling of the improbable and the mundane!"

That the novelist is not punctilious regarding the observance of chronology is also evident on the very first page of the book.

There is a frequent forward or backward shift in time that makes it to trace the proper sequence of events in the life of the protagonist. What the publisher's blurb[12] says of Rushdie's book *The Satanic Verses*, we can say of his *Midnight's Children*, too "the past and the future chase each other furiously." At the very outset, after having given the date of his birth, the narrator somersaults to his thirty-first birthday. He then dives deep into the past only to return to the present, and then to embark upon the future. He feels that it is incumbent upon him "to write the future as I have written the past." (462)

This marked break in chronology in the novel reveals the author's intention of giving not a record of events in the order of their occurrence but of projecting the basic historical truth as interacting with and affecting the life of the individual, that is, chiefly, the author himself as represented by the protagonist. On the one side we have Saleem's personal life, and, on the other, corresponding to this is the life and history of the nation. The story traces the various events in the life of the central character that synchronize with major happenings in the recent history of India. The parallel that is worked out, though strained at times, is designed to allow an understanding of the individual's life in terms of historical forces.

Also, one cannot but note that all through the novel Rushdie is preoccupied with a quest for identity and is impatient to gain an insight into the "meaning" of life. He has definitely launched out to search for the purpose of existence. "I must work faster," his protagonist tells us," if I am to end up meaning—yes meaning—something." (9) And again, "Am I so far gone in my desperate need for meaning, that I am prepared to distort everything?" (166) Later in the novel, there is a reference to "Saleem, with his desperation for meaning." (356) Such indicators in the narrative leave us in no doubt as to what the writer, consciously or unconsciously, has set out to accomplish in his work. And, if we are to take D.H. Lawrence's advice, we would, instead of trusting the artist, "trust the tale,"[13] and construe timings in the light of whatever evidence there is in the work itself.

Returning, then, to the first of the significant aspects of the novel, there is no gainsaying the fact that Rushdie has ingeniously coupled the autobiographical with the fictional narrative. The narrator-protagonist, Saleem Sinai, prepares us at the very outset for just such a fusion when he writes of this "excess of intertwined lives events miracles places rumours." (9) The element of fantasy in the novel is introduced in such a matter-of-fact way that the reader swallows it almost unquestioningly through he knows quite well that this is one of those extra-historical factors in the novel that lend it interest rather than authenticity. In fact, the juxtaposition of the two contrastive elements of fantasy[14] and reality[15] has been so skilfully effected in the narrative that one is left not with a sense of incongruity but with the consciousness of a comprehensive general design in which the magical and real shade off into each other very naturally, the former bringing into relief the historical truth the writer sets out to explore and fix.

Rushdie's protagonist talks about "the mind's divisions between fantasy and reality" (167) but in the novel itself no such divisions seem to exist for both these constituents jointly contribute towards the aesthetic realization of the author's as well as his narrator's "urge to encapsulate the whole of reality." (75) We have the symbolic Lifafa Das, the peep show man, who tries to capture "the whole of reality" in his box. Thus, the fantastic here is not merely "the occult, the inexplicable telepathy, people disappearing in baskets, and so on"[16] it is essentially strategic in nature in the sense that it becomes a fictional mode of projecting reality and offers the real in terms of the fanciful and the bizarre.

Certain observations made in the course of the novel reveal Rushdie's attitude to reality, and bring home the message that the novelist's truth is different from that of the historian. "Sometimes legends make reality and become more useful than the facts,"(47) says Rushdie's narrator in trying to bring out the nature of fictional reality. And, again: "Reality can have metaphorical content; that does not make it less real." (200) It is clear that Rushdie's treatment of history is in conformity with his idea of "illusory fictional reality,"[17] which while recording historical truth does not insist upon a total transcription of reality.

Midnight's Children themselves are metaphorically conceived in that they can be made to represent many things. The author himself suggests this:

> They can be seen as the last throw of everything antiquated and retrogressive in our myth-ridden nation, whose defeat was entirely desirable in the context of a modernizing twentieth century economy; or as the true hope of freedom which is now forever extinguished; but what they must not become is the bizarre creation of a rambling diseased mind. (200)

It is this "quality of visionary insight"[18] created by Rushdie's use of metaphors and symbols that lends distinction to his work.

Apart from the metaphorical value that the midnight's children have, each one of them has also been endowed with certain magical traits:

> What made the events noteworthy was the nature of these children every one of whom was, through some freak of biology, or perhaps owing to some preternatural power of the moment or just conceivably by sheer coincidence, endowed with features, talents and faculties which can only be described as miraculous. (195)

The supernatural qualities ascribed to these children are the author's means of lending validity to his protagonist's omniscience. Saleem's power of telepathy and the voices speaking inside his head enable him to provide the missing links in the narrative and to maintain the continuity of the story for "most of what matters in our lives takes place in our absence." (19) Besides, even "memory cracks beyond hope of reassembly." (384) There are "fadings" and "gaps" and hence it is "necessary to improvise on occasion" (384)—"the trick is to fill in the gaps." (427)

The providing of miraculous powers to the children born on the midnight of Independence also enables the novelist to expatiate upon the superhuman traits of the mythic Hindu heroes by comparing his "midnight's children" with these prodigies:

> So among the Midnight's Children were infants with powers of transmutation, flight, prophecy and wizardry . . . but two of us were born on thc stroke of midnight. Saleem and Shiva . . . to Shiva the hour had given the gifts of war (of Ram who could draw the undrawable bow; of Arjuna and Bhima, the ancient prowess of Kurus and Pandava united unstoppably in him!). (200)

Saleem himself refers to his "miraculous nature, which involved me beyond all mitigation in the myth life of India." (244)

Rushdie's sense of fantasy seen in his prolific inventiveness[19] and comic approach pervades his entire art of novel writing but it is never allowed to exist without the surer base of realism which lends the world of the book a truth of its own. It is his "bivision of fact and fantasy,"[20] then, that strikes the balance. Rushdie's defence of his use of fantasy in *The Satanic Verses* is equally applicable to *Midnight's Children*: "I genuinely believed that my overt use of fabulation would make it clear to any reader that I was not attempting to falsify history, but to allow a fiction to take off from history."[21] Elsewhere in the same article, Rushdie explains: "Fiction uses facts as the starting place and then spirals away to explore its concerns, which are only tangentially historical." (92)

In *Midnight's Children* Rushdie has ingeniously demonstrated his ability to historify myth and fictionalize history. His most potent message in the novel, as Nancy E. Batty points out, is that "if history is composed of fictions, then fiction can be composed of history."

In this regard it is noteworthy that in *Midnight's Children* the degree of fantasy introduced varies with the extent of his acquaintance with facts. He indulges in fantasy when he is ignorant or unsure of facts—to fill in the "gaps," as the narrator tells us. His Pakistan is more of a fantasy[22] than reality and he himself admits it with characteristic casualness: "Anyway, it was not 'my' country" (291) he makes his protagonist in the novel say. It is, however, not true that he did not know enough about Pakistan for he does give us in a nutshell a fairly authentic history of that nation and he also tries to establish "connections" with that country; for example, we hear Saleem say, "I helped to change the fate of the land of the Pure" (287) and "with the Fate of the nation in my hand." (290) But, he certainly knew much more about India, the country of his birth, and, at certain unguarded moments, his emotional ties clearly reveal themselves. In one of his interviews, Rushdie tells us about *Midnight's Children*:

> Well, I suppose, it began by being a novel of memory. The original motivation was to write about my childhood home, Bombay at the time when I was growing up there.[23]

This original motivation, however, took on larger implications and the work came to be a literary exploration of "the memory of a society in political and social decline."[24]

Rushdie's blending of fiction and fact we see also in the especial way in which he portrays imaginary people—though some of his characters are clearly identifiable—reacting to real events. The result again is the desired one: a kind of mythicized history, a work that conveys more the feeling than the facts of the period, though the basic limits imposed by history are never entirely violated.

The "real" events that Rushdie depicts are not mere concrete incidents tracing the political history of India from the pre-independence days to the present times; they comprise the complex of events and situations that is certainly not quantifiable.[25] *Midnight's Children* does not reveal the movement of history in vividly realized concrete occurrences given in their chronological order, nor does it depend on meticulous details. In fact, as we have already seen, there is a marked break in chronology and this is significant in revealing the novelist's intention and design. The novel is not meant to be a bald chronological account of the period portrayed. It concentrates on projecting the kind of fuller historical truth that incorporates the social and historical reality of the times as interacting with, and affecting, the life of the individual, that is chiefly the protagonist himself who undoubtedly represents the author.

On the other band, the imaginary characters portrayed are indicative of the novelist's indulgence in fantasy and imagination. All the "midnight's children" have been endowed with certain magical powers and it is through them that we learn to accept the fantastic in the novel. The other characters, too, range from the absolutely human to the strikingly superhuman, from man in general to witches and wizards. Interestingly, while Rushdie's men are not without the power to crystallize the drops of blood coming out of their nostrils into rubies, the inmates of the magicians' ghetto are not devoid of human feelings and sentiments.

So, Rushdie in *Midnight's Children* has made of history "an amazing pot-pourri of clever tricks."[26] He has framed his own "literary aesthetic truth telling"[27] which skilfully incorporates factual as well experiential truth.[28] He has availed himself of the artist's license to take certain imaginative liberties in his work with the intention of giving narrative shape to recorded facts. He re-enacts the past in terms of recognizable constructs and configurations and in doing so, he "allows himself the freedom to weed out pure facts or events, to twist facts, as long as the final view of history does not contradict what happened in the larger scheme."[29]

Rushdie, clearly represented by Saleem the narrator of his novel, makes of his childhood memories a powerful creative force[30] and in writing about his own life and that of his nation, he chooses the vantage point of the present and his mind delves deep into the past giving the tale a historical perspective.

Waghmare, in assessing Chinua Achebe's vision of the past, discusses the novelist's assumption of the part of a biographer:

> When a novelist deals with the past of his own people or community, he has to assume the role of a biographer. A biographer, as Andre Maurois points out, has two duties: he must be a portrait painter and a historian (Maurois, 1960: 30), As an historian he should discover the cultural heritage of his people and chronicle all the important events that might have changed the destiny and

> moulded the social pattern of his people. . . . Soon he realizes that the past of his people or community is his own past in a way.[31]

Rushdie, too, in chronicling his own past and that of his people takes on the mantle of a biographer and performs his "duties" effectively, that is the duty of a portrait painter as well as that of an historian. The work, however, becomes easier when he reminds himself of the parallel drawn by Henry James between the art of the painter and that of the novelist—"as the picture is reality, so the novel is history."[32] It is not enough to offer the reader a mere journalistic reproduction. As Howell puts its, "when realism becomes false to itself, when it heaps up fact merely, and maps life instead of picturing it, realism will perish, too."[33] Rushdie is well aware of this aspect of the art of the novelist as historian. He avoids piling up facts and making his work only a mirror of the times. His is not a mere conventional chronological narration of history but there certainly is a forward linear movement in the account that traces the history of the protagonist and his "twin," the nation, from the pre-Independence days, through the attainment of Independence to the recent times. The telescoping of time and the condensation of space is noteworthy. Also, the novel certainly does have an irreversible linear progression which K. Raghavendra Rao fails to identify. When Rao ventures to say, "Indeed the novel can be read backward without any essential loss of direction or location," obviously, he has failed to appreciate the informing principle underlying the narrative structure. Besides, history, irrespective of how much of it is given to us through the novel, can never be traced backward for it is characterized by an irreversible forward movement. Linked to history, the growth of the protagonist as well as that of the nation is seen as a process. There is no going back. That the novel is autobiographical in content is evident from what Salman-Saleem says in the course of the story telling: "I reach the end of my long-winded autobiography; in words and pickles, I have immortalized my memories." (459)[34] Saleem, at the time of narration, is working in a pickle factory and in writing this saga hopes that

> one day, perhaps, the world may taste the pickles of history. They may be too strong for some palates, their smell may be overpowering, tears may rise to the eyes; I hope nevertheless that it will be possible to say of them that they possess the authentic taste of truth. (461)

He clarifies his stand further and warns us against unsuspecting faith in his version of factuality—"distortions are inevitable in both methods (i.e. words and pickles). We must live, I am afraid, with the shadows of imperfection."(459)[35] Elsewhere he writes, "I remain conscious that errors have already been made . . . the risk of unreliability grows" (270) but "in autobiography, as in all literature, what actually happened is less important than what the author can manage to persuade his audience to believe." (270) So, autobiography is not totally reliable, authentic history, yet it is made convincing by a parallel narration of the biography of the members of Saleem's family and of the concomitant reconstruction of the history of the nation. Saleem himself refers to the probability of his being "only the first historian to write the story of my undeniably exceptional life and times." (295)

Regarding the break in chronology in *Midnight's Children*, it is evident from very beginning that the author never had in mind a sustained biographical account of the life of the protagonist or a record of historical events in order of time. As he himself tells us, his purpose in writing the novel was to focus on "the connection between public affairs and private lives." As he elaborates, "You cannot separate the two. They interpenetrate and that is how the writer needs to examine them, the tint in the context of the other."[36] It is with this objective of examining "one in the context of the other" in view that Rushdie concentrates on the junctural events in the life of Saleem as well as that of the nation. In the novel, on the one side we have Saleem's personal life, and on the other corresponding to this, is the life of the nation. Yet, in the lives of both, only those events which demonstrate the interaction of the two have been selected. The story traces the various crises in the life of the protagonist that synchronize with the major events and movements in the history of modern India—the Jallianwala Bagh tragedy, the Quit India Movement, the Cabinet Mission, the struggle for Independence, the role of the Muslim League, the post-Independence riots, The Five year plans, the re-organization of the states in India, the language agitation, the Chinese aggression, the theft of the sacred relic from Hazratbal mosque, the war with Pakistan, the Independence of Bangla Desh, the Emergency and other historical landmarks. This varied experience including the ordeal of the freedom movement, became, as Shyam M. Asnani puts it, "a part of the life of almost ail the sensitive and enlightened Indians."[37]

Saleem, from the very beginning, as he himself tells us, is conscious of his "centrality' in giving direction to the major events in the history of the nation. At one point in time, much later in life, he even considers himself a "competitor for centrality" (420) along with Indira Gandhi, who was perhaps unaware of the role of the mirror-of-the-nation bestowed on Saleem by her father, Jawahar Lal Nehru, in his letter to Baby Saleem. (122)[38] In fact, in the novel, Saleem's life is the microcosm that reflects and affects the macrocosmic life of the state and reverberates with the impact of the happenings that plague the latter. Saleem is born at midnight on August 15, 1947, the very moment at which India attained her Independence. He is one of the thousand and one midnight's children who are also "the children of the time; fathered . . . by history." (118) The child and the nation go through parallel experiences of the pangs of birth, the caprices of childhood, the traumas of adolescence and the uncertainties of adulthood. As a consequence of the coincidence of his birth and the consistency of this synchrony between his life and the nation's, Saleem becomes "heavily embroiled in Fate" and is "mysteriously handcuffed to history," his destinies "indissolubly chained" to those of his country. (9) He is conscious throughout of his "historical role" (86) for on his shoulders is placed the mantle of being "the newest bearer of that ancient face of India which is also eternally young" (122) and of mirroring the life of the nation. But his historical role does not merely mark him out as the recipient of the impact of historical events; his own personal realities in life often direct the course of history[39]: "already my very presence is having an effect on history, already Baby Saleem is working changes on people around him." (130) And, this continues consistently enough to make one acquiesce in Saleem's observation at the close of the novel: "It is the privilege and the curse of midnight's children to be both masters and victims of their times." (463)

At a critical time in the history of the "child-nation" (172) when, Five-year plans are being charted and elections are in the offing, when language marchers are vociferously demanding the division of Bombay according to linguistic boundaries, the nine-year old Saleem acquires the miraculous gift of telepathy by which he can enter into the minds of people, "tune" (168) his inner ear to their inside-voices to learn their secrets. This "eaves-dropping" (173) on people he knew is Saleem's first entry into the public affairs of India:

> I paradoxically took my first tentative steps towards that involvement with mighty events and public lives from which I would never again be free . . . never, until the Widow . . . (173)

And, henceforth, every event in Saleem's life is linked with some incident in the life of the nation. The elections of 1957 take place before his tenth birthday. A little after his eleventh birthday, "at the end of the year of accelerated history," (241) Saleem attains his full adult height and then, in the elections of 1962, just as 'status quo' is maintained in India, so nothing changes in Saleem's life, too. On December 16, 1971, when Saleem, after his period of exile in Pakistan, returns to India, concealed in Parvati's wicker-basket, Mrs. Gandhi is celebrating her fresh lease of life in Indian politics, for her new Congress party now holds more than two-thirds majority in the National Assembly. In a fit of rage, Saleem resolves to give the nation as he had given himself, the right to choose a better future, for he looks upon the country as "not only my twin-in-birth but also joined to me (so to speak) at the hip, so that what happened to either of us, happened to us both." (385)

At this juncture in the life of both Saleem and the nation, the pace of history accelerates and there are a number of synchronous events on either side. Shiva's "explosion" (410) into the life of Saleem at the magician's ghetto coincides with India's surprising nuclear capability demonstrated with the first nuclear explosions in the deserts of Rajasthan on 18 May 1974. The wedding celebrations of Saleem and Parvati synchronize with the Republic Day festivities in the country and from then onward, the parallels drawn between the life of the protagonist and that of the nation continue through Parvati alias Laylah Sinai; at the time that Lylah enters labour, Indira Gandhi is found guilty of malpractices in the previous elections; Laylah's son, Aadam Sinai, is born on 15 June 1975, the day the Emergency was imposed in India; he, too, like Saleem, is "mysteriously handcuffed to history" (420) and his fortunes are inseparably linked with those of his country; his distress caused by tuberculosis is suspected of having "something darkly metaphorical" in it; it seems to be a manifestation of his "connection-to-history." (422)

> . . . believing that, in those midnight months when the age of my connection-to-history overlapped with his, our private emergency was not unconnected with the larger macrocosmic disease, under whose influence the sun had become as pallid and diseased as our son. (422)

And then, history narrowed down to this final full point!" (436)—Saleem is arrested and imprisoned, he loses his freedom and significantly enough he loses with it his silver spittoon swallowed by bulldozers to sever him from "the last object connecting me to my more tangible, historically verifiable past." (432) Saleem is given no reason for his incarceration, for "Who of all thirty thousand or quarter of a million was told why or wherefore? Who needed to be told?" (434) The culmination, however, comes with Saleem's forced sterilization so that now he is "no longer connected to history, drained above and drained below." (442) Irrevocable harm has been done but, finally, appeasement comes with the fall of the Widow with which also vanished the ailment of Aadam Sinai.

The consistent equation drawn between the principal character in the novel and the nation is a measure to make explicit the empathy experienced by the former (and his creator) with his twin-in-birth." (385) This is how Rushdie projects his concept of history as interacting with the individual and we are introduced to his idea of the interplay of the two on the very first page. Rushdie himself declares that everything in his two novels, *Midnight's Children* and *Shame*, "has had to do with politics and with the relationship of the individual with history."[40] In particular, Book Three of *Midnight's Children*, he feels, has "more to do with the direct collision of the individual with history," [41] it deals with Emergency and its consequences. History in the novel is mediated through the narrator's consciousness and hence the apology for whatever distortions there may be. Born of history, the narrator gives birth (as creator) to history and this reciprocal creative activity knows no end till he is "sucked into the annihilating whirlpool of the multitudes," (463) and ceases to exist as an individual. Rushdie creates in his protagonist a chronicler who registers in his life the interplay of the public and the private spheres. Keith Wilson refers to Saleem as "a narrator who, quite literally, is the history that he records," and, elaborating further, he says: "He subsumes most matter of public record within himself."[42]

Rushdie's vision is clearly historical rather than personal in the sense that he is inclined to see the individual in relation to the larger social and historical forces that condition his life. In *Midnight's Children*, Rushdie's purpose, as B.K. Joshi points out, is "to relate private lives to public events and to explore the limits of individuality in a country as big, as populous and culturally variegated as India."[43] Rushdie is temperamentally averse to brooding. He does not withdraw inwards for his unhappy meditations. He avoids solipsistic reflections. His is not the imagination of escape, but of confrontation. He would rather grapple with intransigent reality and expose it than buy his peace by shutting his eyes to it. Consequently, some of this tendency rubs off on his characters, chiefly his protagonist. This results in an interesting insight which is revealed in Rushdie's realization that while great events take place around human beings, the truly significant developments occur within them, and that to understand life in its totality, one must recognize their inter-relatedness. Just as the powerful tide of history cannot be stemmed by an individual, so too the latter's will or vision cannot be entirely paralyzed by history and his personal life is of interest in itself. It is this belief that makes Rushdie observe that "the small individual lives of men are preferable to all this inflated macrocosmic activity." (435)

Rushdie has, perhaps, carried this parallel between the life of the protagonist with the life of the nation a little too far, but then the matrix of events embroiling both the individual and the state has been so designed as to allow an understanding of the individual primarily in terms of the historical forces that operate in his life.[44] In his efforts to discover the "modes-of-connection," the writer may have stretched his imagination to excess but we may forgive him this as his attempt at understanding the history of the nation is only a strategy for a comprehension of the self.[45] He declares: "I am what I am only in relation to those about me." and his "those" together comprise "the other"[46] in relation to whom we see ourselves. One can have a sense of continuity on the wide map of history which is not easy to perceive in one's life because a nation's history encompasses far more space and time and can be studied on a much larger scale than an individual's. Moreover, the far greater range of history and its multiple perspectives afford a more complete understanding of the challenges an individual has to face and his capabilities to cope with them.

There is yet another advantage of implicating history in one's fate. As we know, proximity to an event tends to cause a loss of perspective. So Rushdie's use of history in an attempt to understand his own life may be seen as an appropriate distancing device. As he explains in the novel:

> Reality is a question of perspective; the further you get from the past, the more concrete and plausible it seems—but as you approach the present, it inevitably seems more and more incredible. (165)

And when we are too close to what is happening, "perspective is impossible . . . we're too close to the cinema screen, the picture is breaking up into dots." So, in the absence of a proper perspective "only subjective judgements are possible." (435) One delves into the past, therefore, to understand the present in terms of the bygones and through indirections to find directions.

It needs to be admitted that even when the past is evoked, it is punctuated by intermittent references to the present to remind us where we are in point of time and to maintain the proper perspective. Padma's presence as "narratee" and as Saleem's "necessary ear" (149) in any recountal of the past is indication enough of the point of view of the narrator. This point of view undergoes several shifts in the course of the novel. Chronology thus remains sacrificed to perspective.

Rushdie's treatment of history is probably a matter of scale. This may have decided his choice of setting one up against the other—the narrowly individual against the broadly public. Besides, the consistent parallel drawn between the individual and the sub-continent is also a deliberate aesthetic choice that helps the writer set the parameters of the plot structure of the novel and give it form. Form is important; nay, inevitable. As Rushdie observes: "Everything has a shape if you look for it. There is no escape from form." (226)

Walter Allen speaks of contemporary novels as "the mirror of the age," a special kind of mirror reflecting "not merely the external features of the age but also its innerface, its nervous system, coursing of its blood and the unconscious prompting and conflicts which sway it."[47] *Midnight's Children*, too, is a mirror reflecting "the deeper stirrings" (18) of the life of the times. Saleem's life, which *is* the novel, is sketched in metaphoric relation to the life of the nation. Aroused into analysis by the contents of the Prime Minister's letter, written to him at the time of his birth—"Your life will be, in a sense, the mirror of our own" (238)—Saleem is set thinking as to "How, in what terms, may the career of a single individual be said to impinge on the fate of a nation?" (238) And then, after strained thought comes the enlightenment, and the "modes-of-connection" are established:

> I must answer in adverbs and hyphens: I was linked to history both literally and metaphorically, both actively and passively, in what our (admirably modern) scientists might term 'modes-of-connection' composed of dualistically combined configurations of the two pairs of opposed adverbs given above. This is why hyphens are necessary: actively-literally, passively-metaphorically, actively-metaphorically and passively-literally, I was inextricably entwined with my world. (238)

Saleem explains further: "By the combination of 'active' and 'literal' I mean, of course, all actions of mine which directly—literally—affected, or altered the course of seminal historical events." (238) And, he goes on to relate how he provided the language marchers demanding the creation of the linguistic state of Gujarat and Maharashtra with their battle cry and thus became actively involved in public events. The second mode "the union of 'passive' and 'metaphorical" (238) included all sociopolitical trends and events which merely by their existence affected Saleem metaphorically, for example, in the reference to "The Fisherman's Pointing Finger" lay the latent connection between the child-nation's efforts to acquire adulthood and Saleem's own gigantic at tempts at growing up. Here the public affected the private in a rather extensive manner. The third 'mode of connection'—the active-metaphorical—encompassed all those occasions on which "things done by or to me were mirrored in the macrocosm of public affairs" (238) and Saleem's individual existence was symbolical of the nation's state. The mutilation of Saleem's little finger had let out spurts of blood; history, too, was marked by a similar maiming and bloody violence had erupted. Lastly, the 'passive-literal' covered all moments at which "national events had a direct bearing upon the lives of myself and my family." (238) Saleem includes under this head the freezing of his father's property and the explosion at Walkeshwar Reservoir.

The various 'modes-of-connection' established between the protagonist and the nation dearly demonstrate the individual's shaping of history and, in turn, being shaped by it.

This correspondence, though drawn too far, enables the novelist to blend the autobiographical, biographical and historical into an organic narrative which carries with it not only credibility and the "solidity of specification"[48] but also a sharpened consciousness of reality that convincingly relates the past to the present and "involves a perception, not only of the past, but of its presence."[49]

Metaphors in *Midnight's Children*, if rightly interpreted, often provide a key to an understanding of the novel and the reality it projects. A prominent and sustained metaphor in the work used in relation to the similar lives of Saleem and the nation is that of the "chutnification of history" (459)—the pickling of time. The symbolic significance of the pickling process is that it preserves time and experience—private as well as public—and makes them available to the generations to come. The taste of the pickles may be "too strong" for some and their smell "overpowering" (461) for others, but they do, hopefully, preserve the taste of truth.

The requirements for "chutnification" are obviously raw materials—fruits, vegetables, fish, vinegar, and spices. But also, clear, penetrating eyes which can gauge the true quality of the vegetables, and a "discerning" nose that can decide "what-must-be-pickled, its humours and messages and emotions." (460) At Braganza pickles are prepared not only by Mary's recipes but also Saleem's special blends which include "memories, dreams, ideas" and which are for mass consumption: "Thirty jars stand upon a shelf, waiting to be unleashed upon the amnesiac nation." In other words, the past is re-interpreted and articulated for those who wish to taste "the pickles' version of history." (460)

> There are, of course, because of "the spice bases," the inevitable distortions of the pickling process. To pickle is to give immortality, after all . . . a certain alteration, a slight intensification of taste, is a small matter, surely? The art is to change the flavour in degree, but not in kind; and above all . . . to give it shape and form—that is to say, meaning. (461)

This is Rushdie's aesthetic credo expressed in an easily understandable domestic image. The externals are no consequence; what matters is the spirit of the thing.

Saleem refers to his tale as "memory's truth," (211)[50] and what differentiates this truth from any other kind of truth is that:

> memory has its own special kind. It selects, eliminates, alters, exaggerates, minimizes, glorifies, and vilifies also; but in the end it creates its own reality, its heterogeneous but usually coherent version of events; and no sane human being ever trusts someone else's version more than his own. (211)

"Memory's truth" is highly selective and sets the limits of its own reality. Rushdie's "chutnification" may be seen as an attempt to blend and mix ideas and events, individual life and public life in such a way as to give life a sense of continuity in the future that he has a longing for, and that he probably feared as lost on the memorable midnight. This explains his reference to his son and his son's son carrying on the process begun by him. We normally look back for a sense of continuity but he has brought the past into the present in order to extend his desire for a sense of continuity into the future. For him the past is not over but continues to make itself felt through its impact. So, it becomes a function of his life in the present. No wonder the boundaries are blurred not only between past and present but also between fact and fiction, imagination and reality. Rushdie dreams his desire into reality—the reality which consists of his life and his country's. The desire for immortality as well as that for continuity are parallel desires, both of which Rushdie cherishes and expresses forcefully.[51]

Another important metaphor in the novel is that of the perforated cloth through which Saleem's grandfather, Dr. Aadam Aziz, once examined as a patient his grandmother Naseem, before he married her. The implication is that narrative is a perforated sheet which conceals the whole, revealing only parts which appear in the nature of "trailers"[52] to arouse our curiosity.

We come now to the third major aspect of the use of history in the novel, viz., the search for identity. *Midnight's Children*, like *The Satanic Verses*, is written from "the experience of uprooting"[53] that comes from the migrant condition. Rushdie himself, in an interview by the B.B.C., refers to the "aspects of personal history"[54] contained in *Midnight's Children*, "A man from too many places"[55] he calls himself. Born in India and living in Britain, he is "a product of biethnicity" which according to Suryanarayana Murti is "the creative matrix of his fiction." (71)

Alistair Niven, referring to Rushdie and all those Indian writers, who live in England but write about their own subcontinent, describes what they would term "detachment" in their works as "a deracinated loss of identity . . . it is hard to see where they belong." Rushdie himself confirms this "sense of deracination"[56] experienced by him while studying at Rugby School, where racial prejudice was so pronounced that for the first time he realized that he belonged to "a race" and "suddenly in England I became Indian."[57] The irony, however, lay in the fact that while in England he felt like an Indian, in India his family felt discriminated against and moved to Pakistan. But even that move failed. So, when he settled down in England, he began to reach for his roots, and *Midnight's Children* became the medium of the quest of one who could never really "belong" anywhere.

Ashutosh Banerjee refers to Saleem in *Midnight's Children* as "Rushdie's fictional alter ego."[58] Saleem, having been born at the precise moment at which India attained her Independence, establishes a kinship with his creator in that the latter, too, was born about that time, that is, two months before the Indian Independence, in June, 1947, in Bombay. Rushdie has deliberately fictionalized his date of birth in his novel for narrative purposes, for it the time of Saleem's birth that subjects him to a more difficult fate by giving his identity a larger dimension. It is as "midnight's child" born on 15 August, 1947, that Saleem, is "mysteriously handcuffed to history." (9) He becomes, as M.K. Naik observes, conscious of his "larger identity"[59] rather early in life. Naik draws attention to "the protagonist's identity crisis," (52) and comes to the conclusion that *Midnight's Children* "illustrates the permanent plight of individual identity in the hostile modern world which makes it impossible for any one to remain an island but compels every one to be part of a continent, with the result that the individual is inevitably "handcuffed to history." (54) Thus, the central theme of the novel, according to Naik, is the fate of individual identity in a hostile world, which causes it to suffer fragmentation and sterility.

Saleem is the central consciousness in the novel whose ordeals and tribulations are closely followed and analyzed. He is an extremely sensitive and self-conscious narrator (like his creator), and, in spite of all other weakness, is confident of his competence as a storyteller. He knows that Padma, who, as Nancy Batty points out, is the "index for reader-response to the framed narrative," (53) will not be able to resist the charm of his narration: "No doubt about it my story has her by the throat." (38) Padma as narratee does offer attention in exchange for information but seems well aware of the "constructedness"[60] of Saleem's narration for she can seldom comprehend any connection between Saleem's stories and his "real" existence. "There is reason to believe," says Nancy Batty, "that even Saleem's explicit audience, Padma, regards Saleem's autobiography as a fiction." (60) Thus Saleem like his maker, is a "creator rather than recorder of his own history,"[61] and suggests that by filling in the gaps where . . . memory cracks" (384) he presents a narrative that is, in the ultimate analysis, tentative rather than unalterable and final—tentative because it deals in "broken mirrors, some of whose fragments have been irretrievably lost."[62]

Despite the tentative nature of the narrative that Saleem weaves out of his fractured *human* perception he never, during the course of the narrative, abandons his pursuit of the meaning of life, though "meaning he knows [as his creator does] is a shaky edifice that we build out of scraps, dogmas, childhood injuries, newspaper articles, chance remarks, people you love, people you hate, old films, small victories."[63]

Saleem is conscious of the whirling speed with which time is passing and in his search for identity and "meaning," he races against time which is "running out." (9) He never gives up the quest for meaning, though he has to maintain all along a certain degree of caution, for, in his desire to place himself in a central role, he is inclined to misrepresent things; this apprehension is revealed in his self-analysis later:

> Am I so far gone in my desperate need for meaning, that I'm prepared to distort everything—to rewrite the whole history of my times purely in order to place myself in a central role? Today, in my confusion I can't judge. I'll have to leave it to others. (166)

But soon, "after years of yearning for importance," (350) Saleem, the budha, who had abandoned consciousness and deliberately severed himself from history, comes to the realization that any determination to espouse a historical role was futile for every individual is nothing but a drop in the river of human life, and yet, human life is what it is merely because of the presence of that one drop and many other such drops:

> Who what am I? My answer: I am the sum total of everything that went before me, of all I have been seen done, of everything done to me. I am every one, everything of whose being-in-the-world affected was affected by mine. I am anything that happens after I have gone which would not have happened if I had not come. Nor am I particularly exceptional in this matter; each, 'I', everyone of the now-six-hundred-million-plus of us, contains a similar multitude. I report for the last time, to understand me, you will have to swallow a world. (383)

Thus, each individual, can claim an identity of his own, and yet, he has to submit to a final merger with the milling myriads who make their respective contributions and then pass into anonymity.

Saleem, like his creator, believes firmly in the ultimate merging in of the individual with the multitudes so that he is no longer a separate entity but an inseparable part of the "many." This faith is harboured with unflagging conviction from the first to the last page of the novel. In the beginning, Saleem tells us:

> I have been a swallower of lives; and to know me just the one of me, you'll have to swallow the lot as well. Consumed multitudes are jostling and shoving inside me. (9)

At the end, too, his faith remains unchanged and he reaffirms his belief: "I have been so-many too-many persons." (463) And he visualizes himself being "sucked into the annihilating whirlpool of the multitudes." (463)

Attributing Rushdie's protagonist's problems of identity to the writer himself, one would be inclined to think that throughout the novel, Rushdie is preoccupied with a searh for identity.[64] There is, I feel, justification enough for this though Rushdie himself would have us believe that he is engaged in no such quest: "I know who I am and I don't have a sense of having an identiy crisis. But people telling me I should."[65]

But, an assertion is no proof. We cannot always take the writer's word as the ultimate authority to arrive at our conclusions for he may be either deliberately misleading us in our attempt at interpretation, or he may himself be unconsciously trying to establish his identity. This will become clear presently. Such close parallels and correspondences between the life of the protagonist and that of the nation can be drawn only by one who himself is deeply involved, and thus finds it difficult to maintain objectivity and distance in his art[66] in spite of every distancing device adopted. Saleem clearly filters for us the author's own experiences.

The central query in *Midnight's Children*, then, is: what is the compulsion—aesthetic or personal—that makes the novelist assiduously weave such a complex web of parallels between the life of the protagonist (who may very well be identified with the novelist himself) and that of the nation? Could it be the artist's own way of reconstructing meaning out of the chaos of the times, of discovering his identity in the context of a large perspective? In spite of the novelist's denial one has little doubt that the work is a verbalization of the writer's quest for identity, his desire to "belong" somewhere and to discover where he belongs; an expression of his urge to know how he came to be what he is and how he came to be where he is. To Keats "what the imagination seizes as beauty must be the truth"; to Rushdie, what the fancy apprehends as content must be the meaningful truth. The apparently fanciful images and constructs must merge into a significant whole. Thus, what Rushdie embarks upon is an exploration of his life, which he identifies with the life of the state, and more specifically, with the life of the particular community to which he belongs, viz., the Muslims.

One admires in Rushdie, as one does in Dickens, the intellectual audacity to adopt fantasy as a means of depicting truth, for verisimilitude[67] and historical precision alone do not seem to serve his desire to project the kind of reality he wishes to. Fantasy allows a free play to the mind that realism would restrain, and hence a balance has to be struck between the fantastic and the real, for "this elusive and profound relationship between history and private fantasy is repeatedly the key to a whole fictional world."[68]

Rushdie's fantasizing mixed with first-person narrative is a kind of modernistic device to stress the fictive nature of his fiction as also to accommodate fantasy to fact to represent or reenact better those aspects of reality that have been poignantly experienced by him and would not be easily captured in words which never fail in a realistic novel.

As Tom Wolfe asserts, "fantasy is a part of reality"[69] but for Rushdie, it is so much more; it helps him rise above reality and "assert seeming independence of creativity as the distinctive quality of art."[70] It not only stresses the fictive element in the narrative but is, indeed, revelatory—revelatory of the mind behind the work. In other words, it is self-reflexive fiction in which fiction is nothing but a mode of reality, the reality of the author's self caught in a complex interplay with historical reality.

Fantasy in *Midnight's Children*, besides being a form of reality, also serves to add spice to the narrative and to provide relief from the strain of trying to comprehend the truth in terms of the factual. It energetically exploits the comic in character, situation and language providing the novel a strikingly fresh and absorbing dimension. Rushdie, in *Midnight's Children*, devises what Kundera visualizes as "a new art of novelistic counterpoint" (which can blend philosophy, narrative and dream into one music).[71]

NOTES

1. Michiko Kakutani "Do facts and Fiction Mix?" *New York Times Book Review*, Jan. 27, 1980.
2. Emile Zola, *Du Roman Experimental*, Chapter 1 Le Roman Experimental (1880), trans. Belle M. Sherman (New York$_4$ 1893); qtd. Miriam Allott, "The Novel as a Portrait of Life," *Novelists on the Novel* (London: Routledge and Kegan Paul, 1965), p. 70.
3. "Raj Reversal," *Sunday*, 4-10 Dec. 1988, p. 30.
4. Richard F. Button, trans., *The Arabian Night's Entertainment or The Book of a Thousand and One Nights* (New York: Random, 1932).
5. Nancy E. Batty, "The Art of Suspense: Rushdie's 1001 (Midnights)," *Ariel*, Vol. 18, Number 3, July 1987, p. 94.
6. "In Good Faith," *Sunday*, 25 Feb.-3 March, 1990, p. 90. Rushdie's defence of *The Satanic Verses*.
7. Salman Rushdie, "Not Guilty!" *Sunday*, 18-24 Feb., 1990, p. 27.
8. Alistair Niven, "Indian Writing in English: Past and Present," Sahitya Akademi International Seminar, Indian Literature in English and English Translation, Feb. 25-28,1986, India International Centre, New Delhi. "He [Rushdie] has brought back Into English fiction a sense of the panoramic."
9. In an interview, Rushdie tells us that he is convinced of the existence of the supernatural world. 'Network East,' BBC 2, Sept. 24, 1998.

10. Rushdie, as he himself tells us, was actually born in June, 1947—Interview with Rushdie, *The Sunday Observer*, Sept. 6, 1987. In the novel Rushdie changes the date for narrative expediency. This is an instance of "fictionalizing fact."
11. Salman Rushdie, *Midnight's Children* (London: Picador, 1982), pp. 1-2.
12. The blurb of *The Satanic Verses* (London: Viking. 1988)
13. D.H. Lawrence, *Studies in Classical American Literature*, Chapter 1: "Never trust the artist. Trust the tale. The proper function of the critic is to save the tale from the artist who created it."
14. C.S. Lewis, *An Experiment in Criticism* (London: Cambridge University Press, 1961, p. 50. "As a literary term fantasy means any narrative that deals with impossible and preternatural."
15. *Ibid.* p. 59; Lewis refers to the "realism of content" and the "realism of presentation." The two, according to him, are independent of each other. Rushdie's, one would feel, is more the "realism of presentation" than the "realism of content" though the contents too may be interpreted at a different level of psychological realism.
16. P. Syal, "*Midnight's Children*," *New Quest*, Nov.-Dec. 1982. p. 349.
17. R.S. Pathak, "History and the Individual in the Novels of Rushdie," *Three Contemporary Novelists*, ed. R.K. Dhawan (New Delhi: Classical, 1985), p. 217.
18. Rita Joshi, "Fantasy as Reality: The Art of Salman Rushdie," *The Sunday Observer*, April 12, 1987.
19. C.D. Narasimhaiah in "Spurious Reputations: Vikram Seth, Rushdie and Tharoor," *Essays in Commonwealth Literature* (Delhi: Pencraft' International, 1995, p. 125) refers to Rushdie as "a juggler of words."
20. V.K. Suryanarayan Murti, "Secular Fantasy: Salman Rushdie's Fiction," *Kohinoor in the Crown: Critical Studies in Indian English Literature* (New Delhi: Sterling, 1987), p. 177.
21. Salman Rushdie "In Good Faith," *Sunday*, 25 Feb-3 March, 1990, p. 91.
22. K Raghavendra Rao, "The Novel as History as 'Chutney': Unriddling Salman Rushdie's *Midnight's Children*," *Perspectives of Indian Fiction in English*, ed. M.K. Naik (New Delhi: Abhinav, 1985), p.157.

23. *"Midnight's Children*—Memory's Recesses," *Northern India Patrika*, Sunday, 16 Jan. 1933, pp.1, 3.
24. "Raj Reversal," *Sunday*, p. 29.
25. Graham Hough, "The Novel and history," *An Essay on Criticism* (London: Duckworth, 1966), p. 114—"We should be wrong, however to judge a novel by the amount of social and historical reality that it incorporates. It is not a quantitative matter."
26. P. Syal, p. 349.
27. David Lodge, "The Novelist at the Cross Roads," *The Novel Today*, ed. Malcolm Bradbury (Great Britain: Pontana, 1977), p. 85.
28. Damian Grant, *Realism, The Critical Idiom Series* (London Methuen, 1970), p. 9. Compare Grant's theory of correspondence and coherence: "the correspondence theory refers automatically to the fact, and requires that truth be verified by reference to it. . . . In the coherence theory . . . truth is not earned by the labour of documentation and analysis but coined, a ready synthesis."
29. William Styron's interpretations on history: quoted in Michiko Kakutain's "Do Facts and Fiction Mix?" *The New York Times Book Review*, Jan. 27, 1960, p. 28.
30. Salman Rushdie, *Imaginary Homelands* (London: Granta Books 1991). p. 10 Rushdie writes of his "urge to reclaim" his childhood years in *Midnight's Children.*
31. J.M. Waghmare, "Chinua Achebe's Vision of the Crumbling Past," *Indian Reading in Commonwealth Literature*, Amur et al, p. 117
32. Henry James, "The Art of Fiction," *The Theory of the American Novel*, ed. George Perkins (U.S.A.: Holt, Rhinehart and Winston, 1970), p.178.
33. Qtd. *Ibid.*, p. xxxi. Compare Graham Hough, p. 111—"veridical imitation of objects in the real world is not the purport of literature."
34. The novel, however, is not to be taken as a sacrosanct version of the life of the novelist for Rushdie himself guides our interpretation of the novel. In an interview (*Northern India Patrika*, 16 Jan. 1983), he voices his opinion regarding the autobiographical element in the book: "It is entirely possible for a novel to be autobiographical and also to be completely fictional. That's what my book is. It is entirely closely and directly out of the city and the places I remembered but there are only one or two characters in that book I would admit as portraits. Probably the most direct portrait is of a

street singer whom I remember from my childhood, but even he, in the book, becomes the parent of Saleem's alter-ego, Shiva, and certainly nothing of that nature happened in real life."

35. Cf. George Watson, "Tense and Time," *The Story of the Novel* (London: Macmillan, 1979), p. 73. Watson refers to a "Wordsworthian intuition that memory is imperfect."
36. Book Review of *Midnight's Children, The Sunday Standard*, 14 June, 1981, p. 6.
37. Shyam M. Asnani, "The Socio-Political Scene of the I930s: Its Impact on thc Indo-English Novel," *Commonwealth Quarterly*, Vol. 6, No. 21, Dec. 1981, p.15.
38. Jawahar Lal Nehru, in his letter to Baby Saleem, wrote: "We shall be watching over your life with the closest attention: it will be, in a sense, the mirror of our own."
39. Shirly Toulson in *Contemporary Novelists*, ed. James Vinson (London: St. James Press, 1972), p. 118, while referring to John Berger's novel, *G*, speaks of the novelist's objective of "depicting how each one of us is history in that we are both monumentally shaped by events, and in small measure, by the mere act of inhabiting our skins, influence their course."
40. Gordon Wise, Interview with Salman Rushdie, *Gentleman*, February 1984, p. 59.
41. *Ibid.*, p. 57.
42. Keith Wilson, "*Midnight's Children* and Reader Responsibility," *Central Quarterly*, Vol. 26, No. 3, Autumn, 1984, p. 23.
43. B.K. Joshi, "It May be Long, but it's Not Overwritten," *The Times of India*, 1 Nov. 1981, p. 8.
44. T.S. Eliot, *Selected Prose*, S. John Hayward (Harmondsworth: Penguin 1963), pp. 22-23: An individual with a consciousness of history is also "conscious of his place in time, of his own contemporaneity." However, an individual is an entity in his own right and should avoid "purpose" or aspirations regarding political life for as Rushdie in *Midnight's* Children observes, politics is a "bad dirty business." (p. 435)
45. Levi Strauss: "self, knowledge may only be achieved after establishing a critical distance on one's reality." Cited by Flora Gojnzales, "El Recuurse Del Metodo'," *The Centennial Review*, Vol. XXX, No. 2, Spring 1986, p. 251.

46. Carl R. Mentley, "The Hermeneutic project of Octavio Paz," *The Centennial Review*, Vol. XXX, No. 2, Spring 1986, pp. 156-57. "We all encounter our own self, our own being in the community of the other." Compare Marxism: The individual is seen in close relation to historical and socio-political events.
47. Walter Allen, *Reading a Novel* (Great Britain: Penguin, 1971), pp. 18-19.
48. Henry James, "The Art of Fiction," *The Theory of the American Novel*, p. 185. "I may therefore venture to say that the air of reality (solidity of specification) seems to me the supreme virtue of a novel—the merit on which all its other merits (including that conscious moral purpose of which Mr. Besant speaks) helplessly and submissively depend."
49. T.S. Eliot, p. 22
50. Rushdie, when interviewed by the B.B.C, referred to *Midnight's Children* as "a novel of memory," Network East; B.C. 2, 24 September, 1988. Again in "*Midnight's Children*: Memory's Recesses," his interview published in the *Northern India Patrika*, 16 January, 1983, p. 103, Rushdie speaks of the novel as being "about memory as well as being a novel of memory." He further explains: "It is about the way memory operates when you recall your life."
51. Cf. Carlos Fuentes, "Modern Literature Conference: The Politics of Experience," *The Centennial Review*, Vol. XXX, no. 2, Spring 86, p. 135. "It is important to realize that we remember in the present, that memory is a celebration of the present. It is in the present that we remember and we desire which are two things that come together in writing—memory and yearning. Wanting. Trying to identify with something."
52. Nancy E. Batty, p. 61.
53. Salman Rushdie, "Not guilty," *Sunday*, Feb, 90, p.27.
54. Salman Rushdie, Interview, B.B.C., 2 Sept. 1988.
55. *Ibid.*
56. Bryan Appleyard, "Portrait of the Novelist as a Hot Property," *The Sunday Times Magazine*, Sept. 11, 1998, p. 31.
57. *Ibid.*, p.28.
58. Ashutosh Banerjee, "Narrative Technique in Midnight's Children', *Three Contemporary Novelists*, ed. R.K. Dhawan, p. 196.

59. M.K. Naik, "A Life of Fragments: The Fate of Identity in *Midnight's Children*," *Studies in Indian English Literature* (New Delhi: Sterling, 1987), p. 51.
60. Gerard Genette, *Narrative Discourse: An Essay in Method* 1972, trans. Jane E. Lewin (New York: Cornell Press, 1980); there is an implication regarding the "constructedness" of all narrative.
61. Nancy E. Batty, p. 59
62. Salman Rushdie, "*Midnight's Children*: Memory's Recesses," *Northern India Patrika*, 16 January 1983, p. 3.
63. *Ibid.*
64. The novel clearly appears to be a sublimation of Rushdie's sense of a loss of identity and we have in it 'the constant transformation of what would be "suffering" into works of art . . . for the possibly higher experience of being "transparent"—that is an artist. *John Updike*, ed. David Thoburn and Howard Eiland (New Jersey: Prentice Hall, 1979).
65. Salman Rushdie, Interview, *Northern India Patrika*, 16 Jan. 1983.
66. Cf. Flaubert: "I have always forbidden myself to put anything of myself into my work, and yet I have put in a great deal." Cited Robert Lidell, *A Treatise on the Novel* (1947; London: Jonathan Cape, 1953), p. 104.
67. Vassily Novikow, *Artistic Truth and Dialectics of Creative Work* (Moscow: Progress, 1981). Mark the difference between "verisimilitude" and "truthfulness."
68. Robert Alter, "History, and the New American Novel."
69. Tom Wolfe, "'The New Fiction: Interview with Innovative American Writers," ed. David Bellamy, *The American Review*, Summer, 1976.
70. Vassily Novikov, p. 18. Cf. Lenin "Art does not require the recognition of its works as reality." Lenin, *Collected Works*, Vol. 38, p. 73.
71. Milan Kundera, *The Art of the Novel* (trans. Linder Asher Faber) qtd. *Times Literary Supplement*, June 24-30.

Midnight's Children: A Blend of Autobiography, History and Fantasy

SATISH BARBUDDHE
B.S.P. College, Paratwada

Part I of *Midnight Children* covers the major events that took place in India from 1915 to 1947 i.e. pre-Independence era of India. Part II narrates the childhood of Saleem Sinai, the chief character of the novel, and the last part deals with the emergency period and the related incidents in India in those days. The novel presents the three generations of the Sinai family. It is the story of Saleem Sinai, born with 1001 other Indian children in the hour of midnight, 15 August, 1947. Of the 1001 children, who were born in various parts of the country, only 581 have survived by 1957. Each of these children possesses a superb magical power. The most powerful among these children are Saleem and Shiva who are the arch-rivals for leadership. Saleem calls a conference of the midnight children. These children are not free from the faults that the adults have: "Children are the vessels into which adults pour their poison, and it was the poison of grown-ups which did for us."[1] (256)

Saleem blames the grown-ups for poisoning the minds of these midnight children. India's elite Muslim, Parsee and Hindu live happily here in Bombay:

> These were the people amongst whom I spent my childhood: Mr. Homi Catrack, film magnate and racehorse-owner . . . also old man Ibrahim with his goatee and sisal, his sons Ismail and Ishaq and Ismail's tiny flustery hapless wife Nussie. . . . On the ground floor lived the Dubashes, a physicist who would become a leading light at the Trombay nuclear research base, . . . And, finally, on the top

> floor, were Commander Sabarmati and Lila—Sabarmati who was one of the highest flyers in the Navy, and his wife with her expensive tastes. . . . Selected by William Methwold, these people who would form the centre of my world moved in the Estate and tolerated the curious whims of the Englishman—because the price, after all, was right.[2]

The Methwold estate in Bombay where Saleem lives is described as "three-story homes of gods standing on two-story Olympus, a stunted Kailash!" (108)

In Part One, Saleem, the protagonist, narrates the story of his grandfather, Aadam Aziz, a young doctor who returned from Germany with a good medical degree. One morning, this doctor was taken to examine a patient, Naseem, the ailing daughter of Ghani Sahib, a landlord in Kashmir. He treated her and later on married her. He got a job at Agra University. When he was shifting his family to Agra, he witnessed the Jallianwala Bagh Massacre in Amritsar. "I confess . . . I have noticed a thin crack, like a hair, appearing in my wrist, beneath the skin. . . . No matter. We all owe death a life." (36)

Aadam Aziz was surprised to see Nadir Khan at his residence, one fine morning. He wanted to save his life as he fled from assassins. He expressed his love towards Mumtaz, the second daughter of Aziz, but Major Zulfikar was assigned a job to capture Nadir Khan, whom Nadir avoided skilfully. In the meantime, a wealthy businessman from Delhi Ahmed Sinai married Mumtaz, later on known as Amina.

Soon after the communal riots in Delhi, Ahmed shifted to Bombay where Saleem was born on the midnight stroke of August 15, 1947 at the time when India became independent. Saleem says that "the children of midnight were also the children of the time fathered . . . by history." (118) Saleem said that his birth was prophesied by a fortune-teller and a Sadhu, greeted by the press. Saleem bagged the prize from *The Times of India*. The then Prime Minister Nehru sent his parents a letter praising him and his attitude. Nehru also wrote in the letter that Saleem would become the mirror of the nation.

Part One of the novel chiefly narrates the events that took place in India from 1915 to 1947. Therefore it deals with the early life of Saleem's grandfather Aadam Aziz.

Part Two of the novel begins with the never-ending crisis faced by the family of Ahmed Sinai. The family decided to migrate to Pakistan. But they became the victims of 1965 war. Saleem thought that he was creating a world. He says:

> Because the feeling had come upon me that I was somehow creating a world; that the thoughts that jumped inside were mine, that the bodies I occupied acted at my command; that, as current affairs, arts, sports, the whole rich variety of a first class radio station poured into me, I was somehow making them happen—which is to say, I had entered into the illusion of the artist and thought of the multitudinous realities of the land as the raw unshaped material of my gift. (207)

Illusion of responsibility was of power and not of any guilt. Saleem was neither innocent nor was the only person who was guilty. In *Midnight's Children*, we observe the patches straightaway taken from history. These patches are correspondingly related by direct allusions to practical politics. The readers are supposed to decipher on their own.

The class tension is portrayed in the scene where boatman Tai Bibi and Aadam Aziz have hot discussion. It goes on when we notice the conflict of the poor accordion-player Wee Willie Winkie and the Methwold household. Saleem and Shiva fight over the birthright of India itself. Saleem puts before us the mirror of Indian history. The reader finds number of episodes from the past which are tied together by Saleem. The fiction and the fact go side by side in order to create astonishing effect on the readers. The tension between the two countries is described in this passage along with other vital facts:

> Entirely without my help, India conquered Goa. . . . I played no part in the acquisition of large-scale US aid for Pakistan, nor was I to blame for Sino-Indian border skirmishes in the Aksai-Chin region of Ladakh; the Indian census of 1961 revealed a literacy level of 23.7 percent . . . and in the elections of 1962, the All India Con-

> gress won 361 out of 494 seats in the Lok Sabha, and over 61 percent of all State Assembly seats. (351)

Timothy Brennan describes *Midnight's Children* as "repeatedly recalling the sectarian violence of contemporary Indian Political Life": "*Midnight's Children* therefore elides an older view of the nation with a contemporary and neo-colonial one, in which national 'mythos' merges with a humanist critique of the 'polis.' The familiar 'nativist' rhetoric of much Third-World fiction is therefore both appropriated and parodied. Although much of *Midnight's Children* upholds within a modern and political mode, repeatedly recalling the sectarian violence of contemporary Indian political life and the class tensions against which any national unity is artificially constructed, it is nevertheless designed to suggest the living presence of India's mythical past, not as 'vital tradition' but as 'false consciousness.'

India's mythical past is felt everywhere in the novel. Ganesh is perhaps the most central of all the images. He is a God of good fortune. From the opening pages to the concluding chapter His reference is there. Aadam Aziz is said to have a nose 'comparable only to the trunk of the elephant-headed Ganesh.' (8) In the last pages, Saleem's 'son' Aadam Sinai is described as 'the true son of Shiva-and-Parvati—(the) elephant-headed Ganesh.' (500) Aadam has the qualities of Ganesh i.e. ability to overcome difficulties. Ganesh is 'the typical embodiment of success in life and its accompaniments of good living, prosperity and peace.'[3]

The character of Shiva in the novel has nothing to do with the Shiva myth. For example, Shiva's 'gift of war' is narrated like this: '[Shiva] the god of destruction, who is also most potent of deities; Shiva, greatest of dancers; who rides on a bull; whom no force can resist.' (264) But Shiva in the novel is fallible. He intentionally frightens weaker people. He uses offensive language. He has criminal mind. His action cannot be justified. We cannot expect metamorphosis in his character. He expresses no regret for whatever he does. Shiva joins the election fraud. The rivalry of Saleem and Shiva may have its roots in the legendary rivalry between Shiva and Brahma. Saleem imagines the whole of Indian history and correlates it with his life and other characters. His impotency (lack of practical political power) is in no way an obstacle to his becoming a writer. Saleem acts himself a kind of Big Brother when he narrates how his mental transmissions had the power of entering minds at will. "No never mind chief, just think of me as a . . . a big brother, may be." (273)

Padma is called Saleem's 'interlocutrix' who plays an important role in the novel. She calls Saleem 'city boy.' The word 'Padma' means lotus "and in the traditional Indian consciousness, the lotus symbolises one who was born in slime and mud but is able to reach out to the higher things of life. In other words, the name is suggestive of the ability to capture the essence of both worlds, the sordid and the beautiful."[4]

Padma's relationship with Saleem is often strained. The graphic description of her relationship with Saleem makes us feel that she is an enchantress.

> How I admire the leg-muscles of my solicitous Padma! There she squats, a few feet from my table, her Sari hitched up in fisher woman-fashion—my admiration extends also to her arms, which could wrestle mine down in a trice, and from which, when they enfold me tightly in futile embraces, there is no escape. Past our crisis now, we exist in perfect harmony: I recount, she is recounted to; She ministers, and I accept her ministrations with grace. (324-25)

Padma is a servant, who is narrated at the beginning of this novel like this: "thick of waist, somewhat hairy of forearm."' (21) Saleem later on says, "I must go to bed. Padma is waiting; and I need a little warmth." (36) Saleem cannot extract that heavenly pleasure from her as he is impotent. He is unable to make love to her but he is not indignant. Saleem is sexually attracted towards Padma, but it is the same monotonous 'cold respect.'

Saleem totally disapproves Padma's aesthetic counsels. He is rather sniffy about her suggestions. He thinks that he is superior in his thoughts. He knows the limitations of her advice. Syllogism of her advice is noticed by Saleem. Therefore, he temperamentally sometimes avoids her advice. Padma is not vociferous. Her strength of story telling is superb.

Padma's plebeian strength of story telling is repeated in the story proper by several characters. Mary Pereira, Saleem's Christian ayah, whose gift of preserving memories he compares to Padma's making of Chutney (252), and above all, by the boatman Tai, whose chatter, says Saleem, was fantastic, grandiloquent and ceaseless (9) whose age no one could remember, whose verbiage was endless and his talk 'magical' and who was illiterate."[5]

Padma avoids any contentious argument with Saleem as she dislikes any breaking of the narrative spell:

> I must interrupt myself. I wasn't going today because Padma has started getting irritated whenever my narration becomes self-conscious, whenever, like an incompetent puppeteer, I reveal the hands holding the strings. (72)

She is an illiterate and she regards Saleem as a person who gives more time to his writing. She feels that she is in a very difficult or unpleasant situation. But she never overacts though she understands the nothingness in her life. Her masterful control over Saleem can be felt when we see that she is Saleem's typical audience. She is true critic of Saleem. But there are certain limitations to her criticism.

Salman Rushdie's *Midnight's Children* is a postmodern fantasy. It is a novel which is confessional, but it is an humble effort to gravitate towards the history of India, though the incidents are not in clear chronological order. There is a feeling of inertia sometimes in Saleem's character. He recalls the halcyon days of his early days.

According to Rosemary Jackson, fairytale creates a world which is safely removed from the 'real' world, and so it never threatens the real world, but fantasy is constantly challenging our notion of real world. Fantasy is without any kind of principle or design. *Midnight's Children* is a postmodern fantasy as it is experimental in nature. The narrator admits that he is 'destroying the unities and conventions of fine writing.' (236) The novel opens thus:

> I was born in the city of Bombay—once upon a time. No, that won't do, there's no getting away from the date. I was born in Doctor Narlikar's Nursing Home on August 15th, 1947. And the time? The time matters, too. Well then: at night. No, it's important to be more—On the stroke of midnight, as a matter of fact.

The phrase 'once upon a time' is a beginning of fantasy.

The narrator wishes to narrate the things in its maximum truest form. But he is aware of the problems:

> I must describe, as nearly as possible in spite of this filmy curtain of ambiguities, what actually happened. (87)

Saleem's dexterity is felt everywhere. Though he promises to reveal everything still most part of the details remain wrapped in the 'filmy curtain of ambiguities.' He knows that memory is illusory. He prevaricates sometimes and his rudimentary details amuse the readers. This amusing state does not last for a long time. He explains the role of memory:

> Memory's truth, because memory has its own special kind. It selects, eliminates. alters, exaggerates, minimizes, glorifies and vilifies also; but in the end it creates its own reality, its heterogeneous but usually coherent version of events; and no sane human being ever trusts someone else's version more than his own. (211)

Saleem's dramatic fragmented style of narration could have been inherited from his grandfather who had a habit of seeing all things in piecemeal way. His grandfather Aadam Sinai was a trained medical doctor. In his earlier days, when he was a young man, he was asked to treat a young and sexually attractive girl of a Muslim family.

But he was not allowed to examine the girl fully, instead the girl's female attendants held a sheet, which had a hole in it. The doctor was supposed to inspect the body of his young patient through the hole. In a few years the doctor was able to know the different areas of her body. But as he had never seen her in full form he was never able to guess how she would look if all parts were fitted together. The intermittent look of the patient made the doctor curious about the patient. The only interlink between the patient and the doctor was the hole in a sheet. This is a link between Saleem and his grandfather who both had a habit of seeing the things in a piecemeal way, never in a full form. Saleem had no pre-cognition, therefore he could not predict anything at an early stage. The fragmented style of narration might have been inherited from his grandfather but there is an instance where his mother too is unable to express her affection towards her mother in full. She loves her husband in segments. Saleem feels the existence of "ghostly essence" throughout his life:

> and above all the ghostly essence of perforated sheet, which doomed my mother to learn to love a man in segments, and which condemned me to see my own life—its meanings its structures—in fragments. (107)

Saleem is able to remember the incidents prior to his own birth. The elaboration of the events makes Saleem elated. The hole in the sheet symbolically clears out many ideas in the novel. One day Saleem's mother notices a dark hole in the centre of her father's body (139). Even Saleem too feels a hole at the centre of himself. (193) At the end of the novel the Reverend Mother (Saleem's grandmother) looks down at Saleem "through a hole in a perforated cloud." (461) Saleem himself seems to have some idea of the meaning of these things, it is not altogether clear how these holes contribute to the overall meaning of the story. The parallelism between and the inter-relatedness of Saleem's own life and the history of modern India force the readers to find out metaphorical meaning. There are situations pregnant with several interesting possibilities.

Midnight's Children, of course, as Salman Rushdie himself pointed out in an interview, is a metaphor. Though Saleem had earlier named 'optimism' as a dangerous virus, he at last managed to cure himself of the optimism. He is complaining and anxious in the novel about the plight of midnight's children. He expresses his dissatisfaction and discomfort about the shocking incidents. He sharply expresses his views as if he has been unsuccessful in his efforts:

> It is the privilege and curse of midnight's children to be both masters and victims of their times, to forsake privacy and be sucked into the annihilating whirlpool of the multitudes and to be unable to live or die in peace. (463)

You may call Saleem hypocrite, eccentric, a pensive thinker or a promising brilliant person who plays a central role in the novel. His rambunctious behaviour is closely related to the statements he makes. He claims he is responsible for the birth of a separate Maharashtra State, for the overthrow of the Pakistani Government. He further claims that he is indirectly responsible for the death of Pandit Jawaharlal Nehru. Relatively speaking, some of the statements sound self-respecting to Saleem. Saleem gives self-importance and tries to establish link between his own life and the events in India. He tries to find correspondences or parallels. He says:

> Born amidst correspondence, I have found it continuing to hound me . . . while Indians headed blindly towards a military debacle. I, too, was nearing (and entirely without knowing it) a catastrophe of my own. . . . While Indians attacked under cover of artillery, Amina Sinai planned my downfall, protected by a lie. (300-1)

Sometimes we may feel that the episodes from the history of India may be coincidences as the incidents in his life sway suspiciously.

The novel is a strange blend of autobiography, history and fantasy. The readers may be baffled for sometime noticing extraneous references or links. Saleem's nebulous ideas about his life and the history of India are correlated by him. Saleem's representation of the midnight children born on the night of 15 August 1947 is honest, open and truthful. His stupendous effort to narrate the happenings from the storehouse of memories are experienced throughout the novel. *Midnight's Children* is sufficiently charged with posivitism, fantasy and restatement of Indian history with a sweetener of Saleem's autobiography.

NOTES

1. *Midnight's Children* (Picador, 1982), p. 256
2. *Midnight's Children* (New York: Avon, 1980), p. 112.
3. Stanley Wolpert, *A New History of India* (London: Oxford University Press, 1982), p. 18.
4. Wimal Dissanayake, "Towards a Decolonized English: South Asian Creativity in Fiction," *World Englishes*, Vol. 4, no. 2 (1985), p. 240.
5. Brennan Timothy, *Salman Rushdie and the Third World: Myths of the Nation* (London: Macmillan, 1989), p. 104.

Becoming Women: Travelling Gender and Identity Politics in Four Women's Texts

SIVAMOHAN SUMATHY
Sri Lanka

become 1. intr. begin to be.
2. tr. a) look well on; suit
b) suitable; decorous

The Oxford English Dictionary

Jean Arasanayagam, "born" Jansz Solomons, a Sri Lankan poet, is of Dutch Burgher origin and is married to a Tamil. The Burghers constitute about one percent of the population and are "ethnically" the descendants of the Portuguese, Dutch, British and other colonial settlers of European origin. Rather assimilated into the other "majority" communities of the country, the Burghers have over the years lost some of the features that gave them a distinct political character, although socially this is more ambiguous. Yet this itself is a contradictory process. While today, unlike in the colonial past, they do not have any particular privilege/concession, either in the representative system of governance or in employment and are largely compelled to study either in Sinhala or Tamil, if they opt for the state system of education, socially those who retain their identity form distinct communities of their own.[1] The (dis)assimilation of the Burghers has a bearing on the workings of how the nation/s themselves are constructed.

I begin this chapter by tracing one woman's class, ethnic, and (post)colonial ambivalence toward the Sri Lankan nation and the postcolonial nation itself; the heritages of "woman" in the postcolonial are intermeshed and yet divisive. Holding these thoughts together, I plot out the composition of a particular form of a womanist[2] sensibility, of becoming itself that teeters precariously on the edges of postcolonial heritages. This helps me set off on the quest of how do women become within the postcolonial feminist trajectory? What are their particular relations to *becoming* in the international/ized trajectory of feminism? The rather specific historical and postcolonial location, which I map here with respect to Arasanayagam, lays the ground work for my more speculative textual analysis of the postcolonial and the international in the literary works of Suniti Namjoshi, Arundhati Roy, and other non-fictional critical works of theorists and activists. How do women become?

Writing during the growing militancy of the Tamil community in Sri Lanka, Jean Arasanayagam who belongs to a marginalized, and today, an almost politically unrecognized community, is married to a Tamil and lives in a predominantly Sinhala area, has a difficult task in finding a speaking voice that will address all of these issues. Her poetry bears testimony to this long drawn out process of "belonging" in the postcolonial nation, of a middle class and professional woman of a minority within and tangential to another highly politically nationalized minority.

Her writing career spans some 25 odd-years and shows a progression that bears interesting similarities with the progression of the historical discourse on Sri Lanka. The most notable collections of her poetry are *Kindura* (1973), *Trial by Terror* (1987), *Reddened Water Flows Clear* (1991) and *Shooting the Floricans* (1994). The increasing ruptures caused within the Sri Lankan body politic by ethnic strife and the increasing importance of the feminist movement, both nationally and internationally, are issues brought together in her poems, signifying and reflecting on what I shall call postcolonial feminism or the postcolonial feminist trajectory. She brings together the discourse on nationalism by looking at her colonial heritage, the war that is tearing apart the country, her own multi-dimensional "subject" status, as part of a minority within another minority, and the discourse on feminism. In this manner, she produces her own subjective discourse on the way postcolonialism operates today. Here, I propose to look at sections from her collection of poems, *Shooting the Floricans* and at selected poems from the sections "A Colonial Heritage," "Another Heritage," "War and Violence" and "Self."

The historical birth of Ceylon as an independent commonwealth country in 1948 and Sri Lanka as the Republic in 1972 are the defining form of the national heritages here. I shall in this section use the term "Ceylon" in referring to the colonial state and "Sri Lanka" when referring to the postcolonial state, as these different names capture a sense of the different historical situations of the colonial and postcolonial stages and have different emotional resonances for me. Sri Lanka, after gaining independence and commonwealth status in 1948, declared itself a republic in 1972, naming itself Sri Lanka, establishing one common official name in Sinhala, Tamil and English. The "nation" embarked on its new status as a Republic amidst widespread discontent among the politically dominant ethnic group—Tamils. This naming and becoming of a nation, not once but twice, is the beginning of its rapid decline from 1971 onwards (beginning with the Southern student and youth-led Maoist insurrection), resulting in its crisis in the 1980s. Today for me, the name "Ceylon" is informed by a romantic yearning for the past—the age of the emergence of national movements and anti-colonialism, culminating in the gaining of independence, a flag, and a national anthem. This resonates with Arasanayagam's poetry too, nostalgic and colonialist, and at the same time aware of what is at stake in the nostalgia.

This sense of historicity is clearly visible in her poetry. The collection of poems starting with the section "Colonial Heritage" concludes with the section "Self," reflecting, quite curiously, her own recuperative journey from the historical past to her current status as an individual. She also connects herself to the colonial past of Sri Lanka, acutely conscious of the genealogy of the postcolonial Sri Lankan state. Heritage is a self-conscious term for Jean Arasanayagam who has seen heritages sprout by the dozen and ethnic diversities, political aspirations, and hatreds tear apart the country, yoked together by common colonial heritages. About her colonial heritage, a poem in *Red Water Flows Clear* says: "it is only now that identity has become important" (85). Heritage she sees as both colonial and non-colonial. The separation of her own background into two heritages is significant in this sense; one colonial, the "other" noncolonial. Yet both together seem to give way to something beyond—a postcolonial womanist sensibility?

Given the presence of a heightened awareness of identity, subject positions and a culture violently divided along ethnic lines, the poet has to locate herself within hereditary traditions to discover a speaking position for herself. "Maardenhuis—The House of the Virgins Amsterdam/Kalpitiya," the opening poem of the collection (1-4), pays tribute to the virgin-orphans who came out to the colonies, most probably to be wives and sexual partners of lower class Dutch employees of the colonial administration. Her colonial heritage is traced back to "orphan-virgins" from Holland whose tombs litter the graveyard in Kalpitiya on the north-western coast of Ceylon, and not to marauding patriarchal conquerors. But colonizing women were not only second class Dutch victims. In the poem "Surrogate Mothers" (15-18), they were also missionary women finding power in naming the body of the feminized body of land conflated with the narrator's own body. The missionary women bearing English names named "the island of my body" (15). My own interpretive angle sees the body of the female and the body of the colonized land collapsed together, binding the histories of the colonized land with that of the body of the colonized "self" of the post/colonial woman.

The concluding poem of the section "Colonial Heritage" opens into the next section "Another Heritage." Titled "Tradition," (36) it opens up the treasures of the "Other" (Tamil) heritage, which has been plundered and rendered nothing by enemies and aliens. While the poem looks at the violence pervading the north today, the poetic voice itself collapses the violence of invading armies with the violence of a long gone colonial past. The loss for her, the poet, is not a happening of today but of a time past. Does she imply that the violence of the earlier time is the cause of latter-day violence? The narrative voice leaves this question unresolved, merely collapsing metaphors of an earlier time with those of today. The dominant imagery of the first stanza is of present-day violence; for instance the lines "carved door shattered by bullets" and "small rooms that once held treasure/ pettagams of paddy,/ safes filled with gold sovereigns/ now filled with arms," clearly bring up the image of an invading army of modern times. The second stanza brings the violence of today and that of yesterday together.

> They broke open the doors, fired on them
> but there was nothing left to protect
> everything was lost long long ago
> the enemy had reached long before
> those aliens had rifled, and pillaged
> those rooms as they did to that dying
> man, whose earrings they unscrewed
> as he lay drawing his last breath.
> Tradition?
> Blood?
> Name?
> Nothing, nothing, I have nothing
> I have nothing.

Although the images of earrings, pettagams (a chest of drawers), and gold sovereigns are the cultural markers of Northern Tamils in Sri Lanka, the poem is not politically specific about the violence perpetrated on those peopling the poem. Nor is it conscious of the possible upper caste middle class resonances of these symbolic valuables. Riding rough shod over these possible class, caste and regional differences, the poem moves with ease from one image of loss to another where the narrative first person "I" is conflated with the loss of land, class, and heritage of the Tamils. This adds to the sense that the poem connects the new or the present to the past when colonial violence was directed against all peoples of Sri Lanka rather than at any one particular ethnic group. In this concluding poem of the section "Colonial Heritage," the poet seems to be sceptical of what her own and privileged colonial heritage has finally bestowed upon her.

This question leads me on into the imagining of "Another Heritage," the next section, bringing the narrative voice of the poetry closer to the present. It also moves toward a common Sri Lankan womanist perspective. Here she deals with the Tamil mother-in-law-Burgher daughter-in-law relationship within a Sri Lankan discursive paradigm and not within the paradigms of colonialist discourse as she does in "The Colonial Heritage." In the poem "The Ancient Woman" (41-44) of this section, it becomes evident that the Northern Tamil woman has a different genealogy. It apparently goes back to ancient times symbolized by markers of traditional wealth like jewellery and silk. The mercantile city-culture of the daughter-in-law bespeaks of migrations of European origin. Both women draw upon images of dead men of the patriarchal order, within and against which their own subjectivities are set up. With the men who sustained their heritages gone, the two women, one mother-in-law and old, and the other, daughter-in-law and young, live in memories of the past, dreaming of what they did not achieve as women.

> Memories, what colour are they, what shape, what
> Size, my hands rock empty cradles and my eyes
> See inward walking through a desolate temple
> Searching for what lost god, calling in a voice
> That has forgotten all those names, I take up
> Those vessels to give food and drink to beggars,
> Mendicants and holy men but I find I look
> At mocking faces that tell me there's nothing
> Left, no crumb, no drop, no unreplenished, dull, verdigrised.
> Empty as my echoing ear. (44)

The mother-in-law-daughter-in-law relationship persists in the poet's negotiation with a Tamil-Sri Lankan identity. "An Empty Temple" (45-46) once again mythologises this relationship. The relationship takes on an elusive tone. Both protagonists speak through a mythologized language that sidesteps their head-on encounter as socialized women. On the whole her relationship with the mother-in-law takes on the garb of one between goddess and devotee. The narrative voice maintains a respectful distance of age, tradition and piety. This distance governs the relationship, even as the mother-in-law as object comes to stand for what could be recovered and preserved as tradition and identity for the poet. The goddess here is curiously the object of the poet's watchful sensibility. The mother's thirst for life has not disappeared yet; but it is a thirst of the desperate; uttered in her wasting years.

> Her son says. "in the village a thousand trees
> There were, thousands of mangoes picked up in
> Baskets. She must have eaten thousands
> Herself then."
> She looks at life now as if it's a dried
> Sucked out mango stone someone else
> Had savoured but denied her,
> How she longs for its nectar
> On her parched tongue. (45)

The goddess and devotee are both denied passions that allow the poetic voice to construct a womanist subject position. It is both authoritative in its wistfulness, and in its nostalgia for "known" stabilities. Yet there is a reversal of it in the final stanza when the goddess herself calls the "devotee" "Ishwari"—one of the many names of the goddess Shakti, which plays upon the Shaiva-Bhakti sentiment predominant in Northern Jaffna. The emptiness of the mother-in-law's room is changed into the image of an empty temple bereft of its goddess.

> Her room is like an empty temple now and
> There's no one to hold incense or burn camphor
> To the ghost of a forgotten image.
>
> Once, and now I wonder at it,
> When I bore, in my two hands my daily offerings
> To her as if I were the last to visit the sanctum,
> It was she who called me
> "Ishwari." (46)

The mythologizing of the entire relationship gives meaning to the daughter-in-law's life within the empty sanctum of the temple because she, coming down in the line of women serving women, continues the tradition of living out the myth of the goddess. The opening lines of the poem "I wash out my mother-in-law's room" (45) reflect on the narrator's attempt to erase the mother-in-law's memory from her life. The concluding lines pay homage to the image of the mother-in-law, as the narrative voice makes room for both women in the temple. Arasanayagam's recuperation of heritage is through a genealogy of the woman, marked and brought together cross-culturally through a certain class dynamic and nationalist belonging within Sri Lanka. It is achieved and mediated through connections with women: in the case of the European, through virgin orphans, missionary women and the narrator's own mother; and in the case of the Tamil heritage, through the mother-in law and not through the husband. These recuperations of history as subjective experiences of individuals, particularly of women, reflect on the postcolonial trajectory, for they engage with the paradigms and metaphors of the postcolonial nation, situate "self" within that paradigm, and render the self as consummately transmuted by that paradigm. They are *becoming* women.

The poems in the section "War and Violence" not only brings the reader to the immediate present of the country, but also yoke the subjectivity and female sensibility of the narrative voice to that of the nation's collective sensibilities much more immediately. The images of war and violence found in the poems in the collection here are somewhat different from the stark point-blank images of some of the poems scattered about in the collection *Trial by Terror.* If it is the descriptive visual imagery that is dominant in *Trial by Terror*, in *Shooting the Floricans* it is the narrative that becomes the translator of issues of war. In *Shooting the Floricans* the discursive structure falls back on questions of civilization. Civilization takes on once again an ominously mythic potential. "The Dark of Civilization" (111-12) written as a tribute to Richard de Zoysa, journalist and well known actor-director, who was killed in February 1990 by an extra-judiciary, supposedly state-sponsored, armed squad, brings together the metaphors of Christ betrayed and of the actor's life playing a tragic role. The plays of Shakespeare which Richard repeatedly directed and acted in, turn out to be the archetypal dilemmas of civilizations.

> This play is endless in which they act,
> folio after folio lies before them wrought by
> playwrights of doom, their ruffled pages smirched
> and botched strewn about the stage
> but now the prompter in the wings
> no longer needs remind you of your cue,
> the tragic hero falls, struck dumb before he utters
> those lost lines, the last,
> It's left to us to crowd the stage
> drag down the curtain
> shout not whisper
> We are all betrayed. (112)

The last line of the poem grounds the poem's elusive allegorical discursive structures in the opposition between civilization and non-civilization. The simplicity of the fisherman who found Richard's body on the beach one morning seems to be outside the pale of civilization with its "dark" and "savage" methods. The simple fisherman is outside civilization and is blessed with God's and nature's grace. In Christian terms, the allusion to the fisherman and grace resonates with associations. Yet, what does the poet imply by rendering the fisherman simple? Does she endow the lower class status of the fisherman with a higher sense of morality that is beyond the rapacity of civilization? Yet, the mercenary executioners too seem to be outside civilized behaviour, for

> Poetry never overlaid their tongues and the
> gift, golden of talents that you had mined
> from those deepest seams, never reached their
> hands, only their pockets jingled with the baser
> metals and barter coins you could count,
> thirty pieces of silver to be flung in some
> rubbish heap with rags and old bones
> like their own spent lives. (111)

The poet displaces the political dimension of Richard de Zoysa's murder into dichotomies of dark and light, symbolized by the figure of Christ, and by generic allusions to mythological structures of civilization. The political specificities of violence in the country are rarely discussed. On the contrary, humanity is lumped into collectives of masses pitted against the saviour who redeems sensitive souls like that of the narrator, possessing poetic sensibility or the "simple" fisherman who does not harm anybody. But still, at the dramatic moment of the betrayal of Christ the narrative achieves the tension somehow lacking in the rest of the poem.

> Pilate with delicate flourish rinsed his hands
> wiped them on Jesus' shroud and turned back
> upon the rabble voices thundering in the public square. . . .
> and say, that only one, that simple fisherman,
> had grace. (112)

The extended metaphor of the betrayal of Christ by those in authority, leading to the crucifixion, develops the story of Richard's death, and thereby makes a much more clear political statement than the earlier sections of the poem which immerse themselves in elusive allegorical images.

In contrast, the poem "The Journey" (113-14) deals with the issue of violence much more dialectically. Here the narrative voice sets up the metaphor as the extremely arduous and risky journey that people undertake from the north and north-east to the south of the country through desert, jungle, and water, trekking their way through warring factions. The metaphors of destruction are distributed all along the poem and cannot be neatly schematized into any existing discursive paradigm. The narrative voice is shared between the poet and a traveller woman who makes the journey. The image of destruction presented in the opening lines develops as a journey of the poet's reflection on war. For instance, the opening stanza dwells on the image of "shelled walls" of "empty houses" (113) and lizards playing about in the courtyards, and moves onto images of ruined ancient cities. The middle section moves into the image of a people going away, leaving their homes empty. It dwells on the empty houses left behind, and in turn develops into the "We had a boat ride like on the sea of Galilee" (113).

The poem tries to capture in its temporal narrative movement a spatially distributed scenario, "a landscape," that connects different levels of discursive structures.

> Two pillars, a cross, a bombed church,
> Guernica, landscape for lost souls
> Through the silence the little cicadas throbbing
> in the undergrowth, ticking like rusty clockwork
> The answer in fractured time, Chirico's Enigma
> Of the Hour.
>
> No one asks, "Where are the birds?"
> Rabid dogs there were and many deaths
> And young widows. Very young. Thousands.
> Conception, Copulation, Love, Lust. All absent. (113-14)

The different discursive structures in these two stanzas narrativize the connections between "Guernica" and "rabid dogs," prodding the narratee to draw the connection between Picasso's masterpiece of the desert of western civilization and the wasteland of the war-ravaged country.

The oppositions of war and peace are also tied into the opposition of man and woman. The woman traveller speaks of peace, but the jungle is full of little men preparing for war. But this dichotomizing does not remain static, rigidly redefined by already existing paradigms of discourse. The woman's naiveté is shoved aside by the raised arms of the little men that "divide the skies with swords of flame." The image of peace moves from the naiveté of woman to nature—the dove whose breast is severed by the raised swords of the men. But whereas Noah's dove bears the new leaf of budding life, the dove here bears the "final" leaf of an ended era. While the image of "little men" may jar, I over look the superciliousness in the voice, and instead focus on the conception of historicity. It is a reversal of the image of the dove in the biblical story. This reversal marks a fresh departure from the biblical narrative and thereby suggests a fresh evaluation of the meanings of civilization, war, and peace and in the final analysis even of theology.

> Reserve the naivety for some other era.

They are all deadly serious.
Those little men moving through the trees
Raising their arms on the horizon
Divide the skies with swords of flame
And sever the breast of Noah's dove
As it bears the final leaf
From an ended era. (114)

The poems in the section "Self" connect the individual's spirit to the spirit of nature and myth. Her journey towards self-discovery, through various heritages including war and violence, takes her closer toward an identification with nature as the unblemished space for the poet-woman. As before, the concluding poem "The Poet" (126) of the section "War and Violence" leads into the section "Self." It is about the poet who is an ordinary woman "walking in the hot sun" and is pushed back into insignificance by those who wield power. But she is also an individual possessing the magic of manipulation—the manipulation of words to form a structure of imagination that is political and ideological. The poet is both an object and a subject here, which locates her within a communal setting and assumes a social role for her. The objectification of the insignificant woman is undermined by the power of her subjectivity and that subjectivity is articulated through an assertion, not of the communal power of anonymous women but of the subjective power of her words.

I watch her
She takes the hem of her garment and
Wipes the sweat off her brow
The thin cotton is damp and stained.

She tells herself,
"I am common
Anonymous like all others
Here.
No one knows that I have magic
In my brain."

This tension between women, the anonymous masses of women, and the narrator's "self" is interestingly played out in the poems in "Self." The celebration of the "magic" of the poet's mental faculties ties up with the overcoming of fear that the narrator engages in, in the opening poem, "Watch the poor scarecrow" (129). The nature-versus-civilization opposition is schemed along woman-versus-man opposition. The narrator's voice, which assumes the tone of a bird's, is posited against the scarecrow-man's form. The second stanza speaks of the bird's harmonious unity with nature and sets up that image against the intimidating figure of the scarecrow in the third. In the last stanza, the self-assertion of the bird, which sees through the "effigy" of the figure symbolizing man, is linked to the poet's own self-assertion as an individual, who is away and beyond the intimidating influence of civilization represented by man.

> I've always watched him from afar
> Believed in, trembled that
> his frightening power would subjugate
> Me.
> Now I know
> he has no secret,
> Beneath that spurious body lies
> This effigy, man.

"Mango Fever" (130-31) captures the narrator's passion for life in its "totality," as it meanders its way through culture, community, nature, family etc.

> There's a devil dancing on the moon tonight
> Masked and the blue snake hoods
> uncurl and rear like thunder about my
> Drumming ears.
>
> All day we ate through stupendous
> Mounds of plucked fruit peeling off the skin
> With our teeth, golden flesh sucked to the stone
> And the nectar dripping from our chins and fingers. (130)

The narrative voice looks back and forward in time, at life as a passionate experience of the totality of Sri Lankan culture itself, as it lives through the whisperings of Rakshas (mythical demons) and devil dances and the piercing screeches of cocks slaughtered in the night. Sri Lankan "culture" as folk culture, reincarnated by the Rakshas and devils and their violence, is linked to the narrator's own yearning for the sensuous pleasures of sinking the teeth into the flesh of ripe mangoes.

There is a medical belief in parts of Sri Lanka that eating too many mangoes at any one time brings on a kind of fever. How much the poet is drawing upon this belief is not clear. But the images of a splurge that have their pleasures tinged with hurt and injury are well brought out in the poem.

> The milk from the mangoes seep out sticky
> On the skins wounding our lips softening
> With ripeness, you prick a hole and suck the juice. (131)

In the last verse, the image of the mother is mixed with the image of "fevered" mangoes oozing bitter-milk, further complicating the total picture of life as one of either pleasure or pain. The act of eating mangoes and feeling its pleasure and pain take the reader through a recuperation of Sri Lankan culture as a "myth" of pleasure and pain. The commonplace of eating mangoes is set within this recuperation. It is "self," situated within a mythology of the postcolonial nation.

The poem personalizes "history" and gains identity through a genealogical recovery of the postcolonial trajectory. Through this trajectory she becomes a Sri Lankan, a translator of its becoming as well. This is most sharply brought out in the comments of New Zealand writer Norman Simms who says:

> She has the poet's imagination and can, even as the madness impinges on her own life and that of those she loves most dearly, transform the suffering of Sri Lanka into a poetry which gives to her homeland—to Tamil and Sinhalese, to Buddhist and Hindu alike—the very dignity the violence denies. (qtd. Yasmine Gooneratne, 22)

The critic here partakes in the same project of producing a nation, Sri Lanka, through the subject position of the poet's voice. Neloufer de Mel strikes a different note. Comparing Arasanayagam to Derek Walcott she looks at hybridity with a great deal of "postcolonial" caution:

> for while hybridity is often posited as a site in which opposite and / or diverse inheritances come together in a syncretic acculturation, it remains a space in which the components that make up hybridity never mesh or mix equally. The burden of complex representation that falls on creative writers also demands that, even as she rightly refuses to dismiss her colonial upbringing, Arasanayagam be more self-conscious of the privileges of the past that cannot be wished away, and the irony of her social (class) position still, in that although largely eroded, colonial history even now locates her as privileged by virtue of her command of English. ("Static Signifiers" xi-xii)

I do agree with de Mel's political position on this. But at the same time I would like to complicate the picture of postcolonial hybridity a little more. The demand she makes of Arasanayagam to be more aware of her privilege glosses over one crucial aspect of hybridity. Unlike the textual ambivalence inherent in what Bhabha calls hybridity, in this context, it serves to question the idea of a monolithic Sri Lankan nation—within the specificities of the postcolonial nation-state. While I may stretch the meaning of hybridity here, I do so deliberately. Hybridity poses certain visible social challenges in the political sphere like the ethnic conflict that challenges the sense of monolithic belonging to the Sri Lankan state. Hybridity in the Sri Lankan context is that of the manifold identities of the postcolonial nation, in which nations have taken over the nation and nationalisms have taken over nationality. But Arasanayagam's hybrid voice, whatever that may be, is self-consciously Sri Lankan, not Burgher or Tamil, and tries very hard to integrate into the national fabric of what is considered indigenous and universally Sri Lankan. If she erases the privileges of class in her womanist voice and identity, it is by investing in what might be considered the interest of a common Sri Lankan identity or of a womanist sensibility of postcolonial belonging to the nation. Hybridity then becomes a postcolonial nationalist feature of cross cultural and cross communal sympathies but one heavily intent on preserving its mythic unity. The class dimension, which de Mel bemoans that the poet is unheedful of is, in actuality, a politically unconscious assertion on the poet's part. Rarely stressed in the poetry, class becomes the unifying feature of a potentially peaceful and civilized Sri Lanka. In other words Arasanayagam's poetry is not really unaware of the poet's privilege. It puts it to good nationalist use.

Her womanism is foregrounded here. The narrative in Arasanayagam's poems draws upon the heritage of multi-faceted identities and their positions in the interfaces of hegemonic social formations, achieving authority partly by belonging to none of the heritages totally and partly by constructing an authoritative female recuperation of Sri Lanka as a nation. Arasanayagam's womanist voice may be hybrid but it definitely does not escape the fraught politics of the country's social movements and dynamics of class and gender and violent nationalisms, despite the universal postcoloniality of her voice. It certainly does not escape the hegemonies of the postcolonial nation and the inter-national.

The English-educated, although small in number, had always been a privileged minority in the country, even during the heyday of the welfare-nationalism of the 1950s-1970s. In the dependent socio-political culture that obtains in Sri Lanka, English represents power and domination, subversively termed, by sections of the under-privileged and dispossessed, "*kaduva*"—the sword: the sword of power and domination not only internationally but intra-nationally too. In Thiru Kandiah's words:

The term crystallizes the socio-psychological attitude of the underdog to all this, of the man who has no chance of beating the English dominated system and of rising by means of the language to the positions that in the kind of society he finds himself in, will help him realize himself and preserve his self-esteem. To him the English language is only too evidently a sword, the symbol of power ("Kaduva" 139).

On the other hand English is viewed by many educationists and policy planners as a link language linking the civil war torn country's different ethnic communities to one another as well as to the rest of the world (Gooneratne 27). This same "link" ideology is *linked* to the dependent open market policy of the recent governments of Sri Lanka under which the private sector both in production and service orientation has achieved a mammoth growth.

In continuing with my discussion of the development of a class structure in post-independence Sri Lanka, I would like to bring in Gramsci's notion of hegemony. Hegemony is generally understood as a top down discursive control of the social apparatus, operating nationally and through the state. For Gramsci, civil society is part of hegemony. But hegemony is not merely top-down control. It operates through a negotiation with the differentially positioned people of the national-state apparatus through a process of consent and coercion (12). Hegemony then is an area of conflict—not only of consent and coercion. Given this scenario and the nation's symbiotic relation with international, hegemony—the operation of the ideological state apparatus of a given historical conjuncture—is understood as being entangled in the struggles of political and cultural practice occupying not an organic monolithic position but a conjunctural and contradictory one. The state and its contradictions are then deeply implicated not only in the structures of political economy, but also in the contradictions of cultural and social economies. For Gramsci, these material-discursive contradictions take on an immense importance in the struggle for political power, hegemony and authority. In giving prominence to the discursive/cultural plane, Gramsci is able to plot even the state as a cultural site, battled over by hegemonic and counter-hegemonic conflict and authority. History itself is seen as part of this conflict of competing cultural groups and political interests.

In one sense, for Gramsci, the state is political society and civil society put together; civil society including the socio-cultural apparatus of the nation-state. The nation is already defined and classified as a bourgeois formation, although it is not given as a monolithic homogenous whole. In this understanding of civil society, the interpellation of collective identities within the nation is a function of social classes and bourgeois national hegemony. In an otherwise fairly positive appraisal of Gramsci, Jean L. Cohen and Andrew Arato charge him with functionalism, noting that it is important to yank civil society from being a mere handmaiden to bourgeois ideology and to persevere in working on and expanding its democratizing tendencies. Gramsci's residual "functionalism" is related to his over-all vision of how economy and politics are in a totalizing position vis-à-vis the state and also civil society. It is tied to how the modern nation-state itself works in the global economy, given the overarching progress of modernity's structures, capitalism, and colonial questing. Civil society's productive and collective subjectivities operate both at the international and national level. The energies of the nation are tied to the operations of international forces acting beyond the revolutionizing agency of democratic impulses.

In this respect, I find Stuart Hall doing a reading of the English nation via Gramsci particularly useful. In *The Hard Road to Renewal*, Hall explores the operations of national hegemony in an economically beleaguered industrial post-empire centre—England. As Hall demonstrates, modernization and modernity are not merely economic processes whereby capital becomes industrious. It is also a moment of active hegemony in which the modern nation predominates as an organizing principle. The viability of the nation here depends on how well it is able to sustain the myths of its unity, of heritage, and of identifications and how well it can renew itself, be born again in the face of crisis. This takes place in the postmodern conditions of Britain in the early Eighties during "Thatcherism," when in the aftermath of its post-imperial economic and cultural decline "Thatcherism" reinvents the myths of Englishness, its superior values, and heritage and paradoxically its project of modernization.

In applying this understanding of hegemony, negotiation of consent and crisis, through operations of civil society, to the postcolonial nation-state of Sri Lanka and the differentiated positioning of the English literati within it, I look at nationalisms, their civil operations and productive subjectivities as part of a series of hegemonic formation of the nation in its relation to globality. The nation/s are fought over in the cultural terrain. Who belongs and how? are important questions mediated by national and inter-national considerations. The heritages of the postcolonial nation become important. Hegemonically, it is important to understand the politically insignificant but socially still dominant role of the English-educated, in the postcolonial trajectory of Sri Lanka. The English-educated have to traverse a path that negotiates with the nationalist paradigms and dynamics of Sri Lanka and carve out a place for themselves within the changing vicissitudes of the country. In postcolonial terms, the English literati act, for the most part, like privileged step-children of the nation and want both to be loved and to keep their privileges as well. Although this is a very harsh statement, the postcolonial trajectory is such that the English educated do enjoy social and economic privileges that are generally denied to the average "native." But I shall also qualify this by adding that this scenario too has gone through a certain historical mutation, with the signifiers of nationality/ ethnicity, social class, religion being rendered more and more unstable by the fracturing that is taking place within the Sri Lankan body politic.

Today, the aspirations of the Sinhala and Tamil-educated from which the English-speaking, fairly elite circle is drawn compound these negotiations. As active bilingualism becomes the norm today among the "English-speaking" social circle, unlike 50 years ago, the political control that this powerful section of society wielded earlier is diminished. In such a complex of forces, the hegemony of the privileged enters a phase of negotiation with the different aspirations of the civil society in the different bid for political and social leadership and consent. Culturally and socially, the literary sensibility of the English literati of Sinhala origin may be more aligned to the aspirations of the Sinhala middle class and even of the lower classes, than to those of their counterparts of Tamil/Muslim origin. At the same time the fracturing of Sri Lankan nationalism into a multitude of social movements today has "freed" the writer in English to pursue her subject position within the construct of the nation, but with a consciousness of a meta narrative transcending the nation and its *petite* quarrels. The translation of cultural and social privilege and consent into political power is always an arena of contest. In the postcolonial set up it enters a renewed definition of unity, solidarity and belongingness.

In the case of Arasanayagam, operating within the hegemony of a Sinhala-dominated postcolonial nation, the privilege of class and linguistic status is double-edged, given her marginal ethnic status. But her poems negotiate with the many constructs of the nation and produce a niche for the poet's "Anglo" voice, which belongs to the internationalist universal woman. This negotiation and struggle over the meaning of the nation constitutes the boundaries of hegemony as well. Writing in the 1980s and 1990s, Arasanayagam is comfortable in her nationally marginalized position, which is internationally valued. Proliferating nationalisms and identities endow her middle-class womanist space with an increased "national" authority, which allows her to make overtures to women of other "nationalities" and "classes" to come together as "women."

The individualist conception of the poetic voice is what gives stability to the "womanist" space of the poems. This stability is delicately balanced within the tensions of the postcolonial. Arasanayagam's poetry constructs a subjectivity and identity through recovery of heritage and history. But this recovery exposes the multi-faceted nature of subjectivity as it confronts history and the political nature of the speaking subject. Her poems are able to construct a female subjectivity, by translating a divided national sensibility into constructions of myth, nature, and heritages. This construction of female subjectivity attains power through its articulation of an individual universal consciousness that negotiates with hegemonic operations of the imperialist-nationalist paradigm. It privileges the poetic sensibility that discursively stands outside the operations of the nation. Yet, because she makes these overtures to differently positioned women within the over-all "nation," for Arasanayagam, the recuperations of history destabilizes the construction of subjectivity; even as she embarks on a mythic recovery of the postcolonial woman as goddess, poet, nature etc. the dynamism of the postcolonial trajectory continuously undermines the stability of her constructions.

The search for identity is crucial in Arasanayagam's troubled nation. In a land besieged with communal strife, Arasanayagam's woman attempts to cut across class and ethnic lines to become women. But the performance of this troubled identity is forever caught within the nation. Recording herself in the contested field of the English language clearly aligned to issues of class and power, Arasanayagam sees woman as a possible transcender of divisive features within the nation. But the nation as an already fractured and unstable category makes her quest a reifying moment of existing divisions and at the same time a dynamic questioning of those self-same divisions.

Heritages form a narrative of identification of oneself as woman, as postcolonial women, within the nation and within the international. Postcolonial heritages are many and are fraught with concerns of class, gender, sexuality and ethnicities. The troubling aspects of this fracturing give voice to how the woman may conceive herself through the faultlines of history. Becoming is a process of how acceptance is woven into the unities of class, gender, nation and sexuality. One may arrive at the closure of gender and nation only by being *becoming*, through national class, gender and sexual considerations in any hegemonic formation.

Postcolonial Genders and Nations

My long introduction to this chapter by way of examining Arasanayagam's poetry serves different but interrelated purposes. For one, it frames and binds my own analytic location to the conflicts within the nation, the conflicts of class, gender, and ethnicity. The subjectivity of a gendered postcolonial self, *becoming*, is rooted and mediated by these emerging conflicts and identities in flux. Secondly, the travel of gender within the nation has inexorable connections to international travel: the travel of women, text, gender and theory. Examining the points of departure and arrival of these trajectories is important. In tandem, I hold intra-national travel and the becoming self of gender within the crisis of the nation in Sri Lanka, as the originating point of the discussion of gender. As I move onto examine inter-national travel of gender and text and its translation in the novels *Mothers of Maya Diip* by Suniti Namjoshi and *The God of Small Things* by Arundhati Roy in these upcoming sections, I want to hold onto those initial moments of conflicted intra-national movements and the hegemonies of the nation in formation.

For Suniti Namjoshi the quest of becoming seems to transcend the nation and in the process throws up questions about the "woman." Namjoshi quintessentially captures the trajectory of travel inter-nationally. An Indian intellectual, among other things, she was an Officer in the prestigious Indian Administrative Service, before moving to Canada and later Britain, where she has occupied academic posts. In her novel, the heritage of postcoloniality plays a somewhat different tune. If Arasanayagam seeks womanhood of the nation in its relations with other nations, Namjoshi's woman is a fraught subject of the international, aiming beyond the national. By placing Namjoshi immediately after Arasanayagam, I wish to explore the problematic of and the tensions between the inter-national and the international together, as they form the crux of the interesting questions about postcoloniality and the postcolonial nation. The idea of the international in Namjoshi's text becomes illuminating only when we recognize the problematic of the intra-national and its configurations.

Mothers of Maya Diip (from now on cited as *Mothers*) is a novel about an "Indian" matriarchy. It begins with the quest for a benevolent and just matriarchy. Playing off of sci-fi and fantasy genres, it sets off to examine the possibilities and viability of a matriarchy in Maya Land. Although the narrative seeks to undermine the sexual and gendered prerogatives of women, still, as an alternative and challenge to patriarchal violence, the stratified matriarchy seems acceptable. Yet, the quest narrative is only a beginning. As daughters and mothers look around for a mother of land and nation, the idea is riven even from the very beginning by a parodic construction of genders and sexualities collapsed onto a map of imperialism and overlay of land. The quest is almost immediately troubled by the specificity of its location on the imperial map.

> Of all the princely states of India there was one in which a matriarchy bloomed unashamedly. Perhaps it was the soil, perhaps the

> climate, perhaps it was the location and the fortuitous accidents of genetic history. Perhaps it was the goddess (whom feminists in the west beseech intermittently). Or perhaps it was the happy line of competent queens. (5)

Beginning with a delineating narrative thread of travel from the "west," of a postcolonial lesbian, Jyanvi, and the celibate Blue Donkey, who is of a distinct gender of its/her own, the text traces the political (in)stability of gender through the examination of a fictional and fantastical matriarchy. Jyanvi and the Blue Donkey go to the matriarchy of Maya Diip which is not "Ma' Deep" as in maternal depths or "dip" but means in the "Indian" language either island/place of refuge or lamp. "Maya" of course is illusion or compassion (6). Armed with these paradoxical meanings of a linguistic fantasy of place, the two set off on an adventure into a land which might make certain truths of the nation and sexuality possible. Both Jyanvi and the Blue Donkey are welcomed into a mono-gendered community of proud mothers, who are nevertheless in deep conflict over the succession to the dominant position in the democracy of the matriarchy. The note of discord had already been struck when a privileged Mayan, Asha the Matriarch's eldest daughter, voiced her opinion that "pretty boys" (male Mayan children), who were abandoned at birth or left to forage for themselves until they fought to death among themselves, "deserved better." Exiled to the forest for her apostasy, Asha constructs another colony of Ashan mothers made up of herself as the chief Matriarch and of other sexually male mothers, originally rescued from the abandoned supply of male babies from Maya land.

In the contention over succession, fought over by the remaining daughters of the Matriarch—Saraswati, Sarala and the poet Premila—the Matriarch and Saraswati are exiled along with Jyanvi, the Blue Donkey and Valerie, a heterosexual "western" (probably white) woman poet, who has sought refuge in Maya Land away from the violence of conventional patriarchy. In the forest, the political refugees find themselves the guests of the Ashans. While the male mothers, Ashans, slowly discover to their interested amazement, truths of patriarchy in other countries, male androids modelled on television heroes from the western world, invite themselves to invade and protect the citizens of the west in Ashaland, namely Valerie, on their own volition and against her wishes—supposedly a hostage. When the Mayans and Asha who have been arrested by the androids fly over land, the helicopter crashes on "Paradise Land," a land made up of a queen and innumerable Gallants, who are in a medieval quest for meaning in romance and service.

The Gallants are adult children with a queen mother and form a gender of their own. The spectacular Gallants are forever in search of an object of love in order to demonstrate their loyalty and commitment. The inhabitants of Paradise Land are the antithesis of the Mayans and Ashans for whom their gender is purely functional. For those in Paradise Land—the Gallants—gender is beyond any value of functionality. Yet the spectacularity of the Gallants proves useful in recovering the matriarchy for the matriarch. With the support of spectacular and purely ornamental displays of invasion by the gallants led by another "Gallant"—Jyanvi—the matriarch regains control of Maya Land.

In many ways, *Mothers* inter-texts with the contemporary international genre of sci-fi, comic medieval melodrama, the 16th century Latin/English political-statist treatise—*Utopia* by Sir Thomas More—and mythic and fable-fantasy, all of which, in their different and yet commonly eurocentric ways, seek to erase history and politics out of the self and the nation. As Stephen Greenblatt argues in *Renaissance Self-Fashioning*, the text *Utopia* sees disciplining modes of self-generated power as a form of self-cancellation. According to Greenblatt, *Utopia* attempts this through cancelling the subjective-self out of the historical struggle of the early modern period, replacing it instead with the paternalism of the hierarchical state ("At the Table of the Great" 11-73). Like *Utopia*, *Mothers* embarks on the quest of the mythical land, which will nevertheless out-do and out-bid history. Similarly, it too is international in scope.

But in another sense it is also a parody of *Utopia*. *Utopia* stands at the historical junctures of the emergence of the western colonialism. Its international scope is marked by the aspirations and limitations of the European state. As Greenblatt argues, its "self-cancellation" is part of an ongoing project of the self-fashioning of the European man on the basis of a colonial "Other." Self-cancellation then is only the suppression and public neutralization of the underside of the self: the other. In this respect, Namjoshi's postcolonial text bears a complex retrospective relation to this early modern treatise on statehood. To the postcolonial woman, the welfare paternalism of the colonial state can provide no easy answers. It could teach only by default. But in setting out to parody by inference the statism of *Utopia* and its non-subjectivities, Namjoshi finds herself caught in another dilemma, an intimately political one for the postcolonial consciousness of the writer. How does one handle the postcolonial, supposedly non-western prerogatives of a hierarchical state, the statism of the (matriarchal) "postcolonial" state, and its modes of self-cancellation projected through anti-imperial, anti-patriarchal, matriarchal conditions? Also, by implication, does Mayaland in any way correspond to the postcolonial state of India and if so in what respects? In tandem, how does one approach its historical limitations within globality, the international? These questions are too many and varied for me to proffer any answers in these pages. I confine myself to talk only about how amongst all these constructions of and resistance to the hegemonies of the nation and its imperial relations, the text tries to pose the question of subjectivity and its resolution.

In the arena of the imperial and postcolonial mapping of the globe, in other words, the international arena, *Mothers* gets caught in its own complex complicities with the colonial text of *Utopia*. Like *Utopia*, the fantastical mode is international; the text undertakes a route through subjectivities and non-subjectivities to aim at a form of compromise between the two. *Utopia* reaches this through the resolutions of self-cancellation, achieving stability in paternalistic statehood. *Mothers* cannot so easily opt for that kind of formal resolution within postcoloniality, marginalized both in location and in its gender. If self cancellation in *Utopia*, as Greenblatt argues, is a form of keeping at bay the radical energy of nascent individualism and yet remain progressive, self-cancellation in Namjoshi's text is more of a productive questioning of maps, nations, and genders.

Self-cancellation here in the text resides in the borders of subjectivity and the imperatives of the parochial and quaint nation. The radical postcolonial text undertakes this by taking apart the certainties of genders and sexualities, exposing the historical limitations of gender and sexual categorizations and their political underpinnings globally. This evokes, to an extent, the performance of the distinctions between a "western" mode of subjectivity and a "non-western" mode of self-cancellation with its excessive and overt politicization of identity in the case of the Mayans. For instance the subjectivities of Jyanvi, who has taken on the identity of a lesbian uninterested in motherhood as a sexual category, and of Valerie, who is again a western "heterosexual" poet fleeing the violence of patriarchy, are beyond the comprehension of the Mayans or the Ashans. These two polar positions within a "female" consciousness is brought together by the Blue Donkey, a mediating category between the two, being neither western nor non-western, man nor woman, mother nor non-mother. The Blue Donkey, with a gender and sexuality of her own, forms a borderland of the national inequities of Maya Diip, the self-complaisance of the non-Mayans, Jyanvi and the white heterosexual woman Valerie, the dangerous precocity and naiveté of the Ashans, and the foolishness of the gallants. As a border figure of these political subjectivities, Blue Donkey helps bring them together into the narrative of proliferating genders keeping aloof and yet helpful, involved politically and yet emotionally stable.

The underpinning tension between the subjective sexuality of Jyanvi, who desires Saraswati, not as a sexual mother but solely as a sexual partner, and the discourses of Maya Diip, which pivot upon an ideological and hierarchical structure of female motherhood, intensify as the discourses of political sexualities themselves proliferate, leading to multiple accounts of sexual genders. The Blue Donkey helps keep the proliferating sexual and gender tensions at bay; in the process, the tensions themselves recede into the fantasy of sci-fi travel with its evocation of performance of medieval melodrama, and with its emphasis on the political manipulation of warring factions.

Yet, quite unexpectedly, Jyanvi who is not of the blood line of the Matriarch and who is felt to be too individualistic, is chosen to succeed the matriarch until Gagri, her eldest granddaughter, groomed from the beginning to take over, comes of age. In this uneasy resolution there is envisaged a possible reconciliation between sexual subjectivity and political motherhood and between the west and the east through the border figure of Jyanvi who is of "Indian" ethnicity and is more importantly non-heterosexual. While the Blue Donkey remains apart, hermit-like with little personal desire, Jyanvi, with her personal sexual longings and yet disinterested maternal politics, is deemed appropriate as the successor. The resolution rests on the appropriate mix of the borderland, a subjectivity rooted in and tempered with political commitment to the matriarchy.

Jyanvi is a cross between a Gallant and a Mayan. This is emphasized in the narrative as well. While she is horrified to be taken for a Gallant by other Paradise Land residents, she does fulfil some of the criteria they apply to gallantry, namely a seeming perusal of pure pleasure. While pleasure is a component of Mayaland (women do form love relationships with other women), this is subordinated to the politics and hierarchies of motherhood, both biological and social. On the other hand, unlike the Gallants, Jyanvi detests all performance of the pleasure-seeking identity. In some ways, she feels quite intact, sufficient unto herself. In choosing Jyanvi as the immediate successor to the matriarchy, the matriarch, and in a broader sense the meta-narrative itself, recognize the need to bring pleasure and functionality together into the production of gender.

Eventually, self-cancellation itself reaches a compromise with the self-production of non-politicized individuation exemplified foremost by Jyanvi. *Mothers*, which initially promises to be such a radical farce of dominant hegemonies, becomes subdued by its own contradictions and complicities constructing an ahistorical universal patriarchy and an ahistorical self-production. Unlike *Utopia* Namjoshi reinserts the self into the text's resolution overtly. Gender is the predominating feature of the performance of self here. In this roaming narrative, the world is splintered forever into myriad genders. Yet by the end, gender in its alliances with sexuality is thrust into the surface of politicking over the succession, ideological correctness, and as a corollary, into a form of self-cancellation.

Mothers as a feminist political fantasy remarks upon the cancellation inherent in any idea of the nation. At the same time, it appears hamstrung by its own fantastical myth making: for instance, the natives, the Mayan mothers of all classes, the Ashans and the Gallants never move beyond the plot of repetitive self-cancellation and lack a collective subjective agency with the exception of the members of the oligarchy and the visitors from the western world. This performance of class and gender together is highly constrained by and reconciled with the discursive international mapping of class and nation. By the end of the text. the performance has settled for a stable human order and an international of a gendered framework. Its underpinning political tensions recede and are partially pulled into the narrative of the reconquest of Maya Diip by the Matriarch with the help of the Blue Donkey, Jyanvi, Saraswati, Asha and the gallants. As the narrative develops through the workings of the manipulative plot of the matriarch, her daughters Saraswati and Asha, and her favoured guests, Jyanvi and the Blue Donkey, the self too recedes, cancels itself, to reveal surfaces of political categories that overrides the emergence of a marginalized collective/fragmented self or of a subjective sexuality. These political categories are of an international order.

Mothers is a text on a rhetorical quest for a language of genders and nations that would transcend the delimitations of the imperial map and its inequalities. The novel reaches a stage beyond the narrow borders of the ideological nation, to herald a possible international subjectivity of gender and self-affirmation. Yet, on the other hand, its (post)colonial ties with *Utopia* are more than those of parody. As a result, like *Utopia,* which through self-cancellation and self-surveillance, seeks to transcend history itself, *Mothers* becomes in the end not the bold critical fantasy it sets out to be at the beginning, but a question partially answered through an inter-national intertextuality—one that resonates through science fiction and a fantasy of global proportions. It boldly sets out to rip apart stable and known truths of the imperial and of gender and unexpectedly settles for an international borderland where politics recede to let an international subject re-emerge. This international subjectivity may be unstable but nevertheless rests on transcending the historical and the conditions of postcoloniality it sets out to remark upon at the beginning. In the process, the dynamism of the imperial map itself that Namjoshi starts off with recedes into political quietism and gender passivity. This dare devil text peters out to be a tame cyclical return to an already stable international. Like Judith Butler in *Gender Trouble*,[3] Namjoshi resorts to locating politics and resistance in the individual body operating outside of the postcolonial map.

Writing about Suniti Namjoshi, Gita Rajan calls her a "specular (border) intellectual, reshaping and reinventing possibilities of the real through her feminist gaze." (91). Drawing upon Abdul JanMohammed's formulation of the border intellectual, who is of the border itself, Rajan talks about Namjoshi as enunciating the border through her postcolonial body. In her words: "She [Namjoshi] is never fully an exile, or immigrant, or anthropologist, yet she always voices the unthought-of possibility" (95). Namjoshi here is seen as a border intellectual and a specular intellectual—a critical (intellectual) visibility of identity that performs spectacularly the problematic of postcoloniality and its attendant social forces, accompanying postmodernity, namely globalism and the transnational. The border intellectual is at the vantage point of underlining the contestations of boundaries and the lines of travel. As a text of border intellect, *Mothers* performs the surfaces of international travel; of gender. But this specularity hides as much as it reveals within the simulacrum of identity. The specularity of the border intellectual poses the limits of the topography of performance; of the speculum or of the itinerary of travel.

The spectacle as the visible space of border(land) contains the multiple trajectories of sex, gender, ethnicity, and race. But the conjunctures of these trajectories also serve to complicate the picture of the postcolonial. The multiple performances of gender endow it with the mobility accompanying travel. In the next section I would like to look at precisely these issues. What makes the performance and travel of gender possible and necessary for postcolonial subjects?

Travelling Women and the Postcolonial Nation

In my examination of Arundhati Roy's text, I hope to bring the seemingly disparate movements of Arasanayagam's intra-national movement of gender, of becoming women, and Namjoshi's internationally wrought text of gender travels, into an embodiment of the inter-national movement of socialized women, one that works both intra-nationally and internationally.

Place, space, and the mobility of gender are the cardinal points of my approach to the text. The novel *God of Small Things* is Arundhati Roy's first novel and was awarded the prestigious Commonwealth award, *The Booker Prize* in 1997. Catapulted into the bestseller list of novels within a short span of time, the novel has gained a great deal of publicity. My intent here is not to study its popularity per se, but to look at the text and the mobility of gender within the nation and the international, in order to gain at least a partial understanding of what this particular inter-national status may entail.

In the novel *becoming* gender is the itinerary of the nation and its women. It is the "quintessential" postcolonial novel of India, where the production of the bourgeois woman plays securely within the nation's aspirations toward attaining international womanhood. It is about the land owning class of Syrian Christians in the state of Kerala, Southern India. While the focus is securely on the deprived women of the land owning and upper middle class Christians, the "woman" question is maintained in the narrative as the quintessential desire of postcoloniality. The text is a re-memory of Rahel of her childhood when she and her twin brother Esthappen, occupying a subordinated position in their maternal grandfather's home, enter adulthood and guilt through a series of events that overturn their sense of the security of childhood, unawareness, and ignorance. The patriarchal household in which Rahel and Esthappen live with their divorced and therefore stigmatized mother Ammu, grandmother Mammachi, Grand aunt Baby Kochamma, and Uncle Chacko becomes in the "realist" fashion, the site of the struggle of history, caste and working class emergences and temerity, and gendered sexual expression. From their very early childhood, Rahel and Esthappen are initiated into the social and political taboos of caste, gender, their own marginalized status because of their inter-ethnic and inter-religious background, and the postcolonial privilege of class, marked by an English-speaking status.

As the fortunes of the land-owning family dwindle, racked by the mismanagement of the family business—the pickle factory, the inefficiency of an idle intelligentsia, and militant trade union activity, the family is forced to face change head on. But these changes are sexual as much as political, and novelistically, the socio-political increasingly interweaves with the subjective-sexual. As part of the historical changes taking place and of the novelistic intermeshing of the social and the sexual, the narrative linearity focuses on Ammu's doubly-tabooed affair with Velutha, the son of one of their workers of the untouchable caste.

In the story, the children occupy a tenuous social space where child molestation at the hands of a stranger, intrusion by a half-English cousin, working class sexual exploitation, gender marginalization and disempowerment and most importantly of all, class and caste oppression and exploitation as well as their emergences characterize the postcolonial specificity of political change in the state of Kerala and in India as a whole. This postcolonial national and social instability emphasize not only the insecurity of the national but that of the children too. They interweave.

The crisis within the family is precipitated by the arrival of Chacko's English ex-wife Margaret and daughter Sophie at which point tensions of gender, class, sexuality and childhood proliferate at many levels. The two children, jealous of the attention their English cousin draws, begin to play at the abandoned ghost-ridden History House to get to which they have to cross a little stream in a boat. History House is also the place of rendezvous for Ammu and Velutha. When Sophie Mol, the English girl drowns in the stream when she follows the other two children, Velutha who had gone over to the meeting place is arrested as the murderer and dies in police custody from injuries sustained under torture. Ammu never recovers from this episode, eventually dying after a few years. Following the two tragic deaths of Sophie Mol and Velutha, the twins are separated from each other against their will by the grand aunt, Kochamma. Estha is sent off to be with his father, after which he stops all productive communication with the rest of the world. After many years, the adult-woman Rahel who has found her way into America returns to Ayemenem to visit Estha who had returned home after his father's emigration to Australia. In an act of mutual need and rememoration, the twins unite in an incestuous sex act. The final chapter goes back to the moment of the sexual consummation of Ammu and Velutha in "History House."

As a postcolonial text, *God of Small Things* is smartly astute in working with history. The novel plays with the idea of colonialism's difficult legacy through the high metaphor of the "History House." The decay of History House has its intricate connections with the dying of the house in Ayemenem, its loss of privilege in the rapidly changing times of bourgeois dominance and working class and caste struggles. The inter-textuality with the realist novel is unmistakable, as it records through interpersonal relations of the land-owning women and their children, the passage of time and an era.

The postcolonial nation has its political emergence as an entity among other nations and as part of the discursivity of international/universal values, rights and responsibilities. The discourse of postcoloniality here in the text makes claim to an understanding of the nation within this construct of universal values. It aspires to detail the dichotomies embedded within an imperial patriarchal understanding of land and history. These are laid out pretty early on in the novel, as postcoloniality seems split between the binary of a matriarchal ecology called "Earth Woman" and the patriarchal colonial "History House." If Earth Mother is beyond comprehension in human terms "History House" on the other hand is very much alive in the children's imagination. History is the dying and yet persistent legacy of colonialism while Earth Woman is taken to persist beyond those limitations. These categories by themselves are never fully developed but are historically transformed into narratives about powerful but also suppressed women of Kerala's land-owning and landless working class peasant women.

What concerns me here is the way gender politics underpins the postcolonial narrativity of a community, struggling to adapt to the political instabilities of the time as four generations of women battle and survive the inequalities of the present, epitomized most by the divorced Ammu's transgressive sexual relations with the untouchable Velutha, and Rahel's displacement from the confined spaces of the house. As women continue to define the borders of community, class, and castes, Rahel almost escapes it by becoming the universal woman, and by symbolically becoming "whole" when she is united with her twin brother. In the incestuous sexual union with her brother at the end, the novel reaches its resolution of becoming a unity; attaining a selfhood which Ammu attempts to achieve through another form of social transgression. The romanticism inherent in the transgressive relation of Ammu, with the untouchable worker, is resolved and consummated in the union of Rahel and Esthappen, trying to recapture the innocence of childhood, but without its inherent ignorance and ignobilites, in another time of adulthood. In this recapitulation the magical coming together of Rahel and Estha and the romantic union of Ammu and Velutha reside almost outside of the political space of the Ayemenem house. These unions move toward the "time" of the forty-six year old "Earth Woman."

Gender and sexuality are the cornerstones of a certain postcolonial mobility, where travel and displacement occur to reempower the object marked by class with a postcolonial subjectivity and to endow the subject with a speaking voice. Borderland and border studies repeatedly emphasize the manifold transgressions that may take place in crossing. When Rahel crosses class by becoming a disinherited granddaughter of a land owning colonial civil servant, or when Ammu dares to desire both in her choice of marriage partner and then later in having a sexual union with the untouchable Velutha, travel serves to unmoor the disempowered gender-subject by granting her the space to move, to act, and thereby to speak through postcolonial history. The woman here becomes mobile and dynamic, an agent of social change leading one to spaces outside society. The move out toward woman, child, and universal persons, also rests on a move toward a point outside of a culturally "incestuous" postcoloniality with its painful but petty hierarchies and injustices.

In postmodern terms, this space outside could be the simulacrum of the social. In the simulacrum of identity outlined by Baudrillard, Deleuze and Guattari and following Deleuze, Michael Hardt, the mobility of gender across the postcolonial nation and internationally, could be performed as travel and becoming. The travel of gender across socially inhibiting structures like class and caste, also serves to unmoor gender from the nationhood of postcoloniality, pinned down by its history-specific social structures. In *God of Small Things* we see a strenuous strival toward the end of history, postcoloniality, and the travails of the nation's difficult and unhappy hierarchies, where cruel and tortuous death predominates as the fatality of caste emergences. In a sense I am working off of a general postcolonial readers' perception that the character of Velutha in *God of Small Things* is romantically drawn and forms in many ways the romantic "Other" of Ammu and Rahel. In this critical context the fatal silencing of caste militancy through a romantic ahistorical sexual union sounds ominously familiar. In the same vein, I see it as crucially important that untouchable women are unseen except as a sexually exploited working class women. When the subjectivity of marginalized Rahel, both when she was a child and later as a disinherited grand-daughter, emerge as a travelling medium, cruising along and against history toward international womanhood and a feminist consciousness, one cannot help but wonder about the desubjectivization of working class and untouchable women.

On the other hand, the very struggle against history serves to situate the text in an uneven relation with other nations, internationally. *God of Small Things* is self-consciously postcolonial, writing within the structure of the international travel of cross cultural professional exchanges. In that respect, the nation in the postcolonial becomes even more accentuated as the terrain of postcolonial historical happenings, of corrupt and dying houses, and corrupt but powerful trade unionism, of gender travel, and caste emergences, and of child abuse and murder. These become the national territorial operations serving the emergence of a postcolonial international gender. In the story of Rahel's and Esthappen's childhood, narrated through the recollection of the child grown adult-woman, the nation is part of an unjust and incomprehensible childhood. Through travel, Rahel the postcolonial child becomes adult and a woman, no longer constrained by the nation of her history. This tension between the two is insistent in the narrative, criss-crossing its "realism" with the "discourse" of woman, of the individual person, and with the idea of a unity, romantically conceived in the sexual union of the brother and sister and of Ammu and Velutha. The final poignant scene, the deferred desires of Ammu and Velutha, is one of breaking a social taboo, but by that same token, it is also a cleansing of the body and its gender of history's messy politics. But this becoming is never a simple escape from history; it also entails a circling back to a sense of the nation in the universal, caught in the troubled metaphor of Rahel's travel back to meet Estha in Ayemenem.

When I taught *God of Small Things* in the American academy, I was surprised to see how accessible it was to young American readers who were usually resistant to texts "far removed" from their "own experiences." The novel seemed to surmount this difficulty when "women" became a theme of classification of identity in the travel of gender, from the postcolonial to the postmodern, and from the nation to the international. But there is no easy resolution here. Gender is never fixed as a universal. It becomes dynamic as it travels. The performance of a gendered identity may not quite escape the postcolonial in its travels. In *God of Small Things* we see this paradox operating almost hegemonically. The dynamism of the travel of gender is driven by the idea and formation of the (postcolonial) nation where the nation is embedded within international cultural acquisition and cultural capital; namely, gaining in one sense, international visibility as the postcolonial itself seems a necessary condition for the global. The performance of the postcolonial in the international arena is not without its negotiations with the international and its hegemonies. In the next section I hope to look at how sharp these discursive realities are within the postcolonial national and the international.

Displeased Women: Displacement and the Crisis of Travel

Travel is an itinerary of a process; of becoming. Travel is presumably a movement through history to a point beyond it. In this respect, postcolonially, the subversive activity of the body could also mean a travel beyond the hegemonic nation. The bid for this movement, away and beyond the inhibiting social forces, is already undermined by the politics of postcolonial mapping. Yet I hope to envision travel as multi-visionary, fraught with the politics of the inter-national and at the same time, underscoring the materiality of *place*, of social movement, of postcolonial tensions of the nation. In moving ahead with these affirmations and dissonances, I hope to move toward a practice of travel, where women are located not merely in the discursive spaces of the international, but also in local and global socio-political place.

Political economy, local sites of resistance, and international travel are brought together in Saskia Sassen's *Globalization and Its Discontent.* Lefebvre and postcolonial activity are also brought together, through a reappropriation of place as a local/global/postcolonial site. Despite my scepticism with some of Sassen's tropic allusions to the global city, and despite a certain expansive looseness about the logic of her work, I find her theoretical narrative of global power relations, micro-politics, and resistance interestingly productive. Sassen to me inserts one of those missing links of the trajectory of international travel, namely "place" as a performance of gender.

The performance of gender, internationally, reinscribes travel as a mediating force. Sassen sees travel as a mediating force in the materiality of the globe. Gender as travel and performance, in the form of subjectively acting on political economy, needs to be added to any Foucauldian rendering of the materiality of discourse. In the mapping of transnational epistemes, Sassen identifies two trajectories of capitalist production against which the discontented operate, not only by questioning its hierarchies, but also by advancing on the containing hegemonies. Using the city and global cities as the sites and grids of transnational activity, Sassen draws a geography of globalization in which travelling gender (among other factors) forms a strategic nexus between transnational operations of capital which need to be studied empirically and theoretically as well as sociopolitically and as subjectivity. For her the strategic nexus "is the transformation of sovereignty and the openings this has created for women (hitherto largely invisible actors) to become visible participants in international relations and subjects of international law"[4] (85). Gender in the form of "women and immigrants" emerges as the systemic equivalent of the "offshore proletariat" (86).

By placing Sassen's gender as an economy of the social against the exclusive politics of self-parody, I hold onto a postcolonial dissatisfaction with the performative discursive space of the body. The body, as Sassen seems to imply later on in her book, needs to be read as place boundedness, which underlines and defines postcoloniality and global activity (203-4). Sassen insists on the study of place and the "First World" urban experience as global activity. In all of this, the performance of the body is important, since the body captures the global in the local and the micro-political. But the two also reside in tension. "Place boundedness" plays a crucial role as it recodes Butler's heterosexist matrix of the nation in myriad different ways, in all of which the international predominates.

Likewise, within the postcolonial trajectory, when gender moves, it is in an uneasy alliance with the privileges of travel. The postcolonial insists on unearthing the social relations of the international. As Edward Soja may say, place/space as the hidden construct of the simulacrum may yet emerge in its diverse ways to thwart the homogeneity of the international and the hegemonies of the national. Smadar Lavie and Ted Swedenburg call it the "third time-space" in their introduction to the ethnographic project of place-bound identifications, an anthology of articles called *Displacement, Diaspora, and Geographies of Identity,* a recovery of "minority" discourses of place challenging eurocentric time. As the editors of this postmodern volume of identities of geography say, identity politics is one in process, a becoming, within the enactment of place, within an anthropological/ ethnographic sense of place. They call for a "reconceptualization" of space, "from the standpoint of lived identities and physical places as well as the texts of expressive culture, of the multiplicities of identity and place," which would challenge the still persistent narrative of capitalist time that seeks to defeat place and subsume it under the subject of the universal (18).

In such a scenario, the "third time-space" becomes a deconstructive venture of travel itself, of becoming, and its teleological drives. But the third time-space as the postcolonial has little validity if it is divorced from an understanding of the economies of place, both political and sexual, and national and inter-national. An understanding of the political and sexual economies of globality seems necessary to challenge and reconfigure social relations and formations of identities within the heritage and hegemony of the international and its travels.

In such an attempt, I move from travel to displacement. In this final section I propose to plot out a sense of place within the absence of travel and becoming. Third-time space is not merely an enactment of place but also a contravention and a querying of place and of the attendant hegemonies of the national and international travel. The idea of displacement immediately foregrounds place as an absent presence. The challenge to different forms of travel is inscribed in displacement, in the economies of inter-national and intra-national movement of women. Here, place as a "third time-space" emerges as a highly contradictory event in becoming, even in postcolonial becoming and identity formation.

Faizun Zackariya and Zulfika Ismail bring up the complexities and contradictions of travel rather sharply in their account of a displaced community and the implications of displacement for gender relations. While the document is severe and unromantic about displacement, it nevertheless attempts to narrate the complex effects and affects of displacement. They talk of a community which is forced to migrate; a community of refugees. After the LTTE[5] forced the northern Muslims of Sri Lanka to vacate the northern province, most of the displaced and dispossessed Muslims relocated in the other areas, where there are large local Muslim communities, like the North western provincial district, Puttalam. Their research and retelling is acutely alive to structural underpinnings and the agency of women who work in those specific locations. While I engage in a dialogue with this text, which is so much part of my own history as well, I do not merely foreground this as an intimate instance of my own story. In a sense the story is not my own. My own story as a displaced Tamil in the South is both alike and not alike the stories narrated here. There is the commonality of war and displacement. But there are also other possible divisions like class and gender. But what is evoked in the story of displacement itself is the difference of ethnicity, which triggered LTTE's ruling to expel the Muslims from their/my homeland. This short document for me encapsulates many of the performances of gender that are inevitably shaped by class, ethnicity (race), region and a multitude of other factors that disallow a free and easy choice of performance, of body and of place.

From the perspectives of Zackariya and Ismail, travel has immutably to do with the social forces shaping one's location. Their document about displaced Muslims from the northern province brings to life sharply the performative of gender that performs the nation and the international at one and the same time. The forced travel of the displaced Muslims, who are refugees in their own nations (both within Sri Lanka and within other Muslim communities), underscore the limitations of individual performances of resistance. The international mapping of the world puts under erasure such a postcolonial rejuvenation of the individual within the constrained circumstances of war, where the nation itself is in crisis and collapse.

Selecting five camps and "nearly one hundred women" for their study, they focus on "investigating the incidence of violence taking place within the family throughout the woman's life cycle, the factors that perpetuate this and how women confronted such violence" (6). For me Zackariya and Ismail attempt to work out a difficult position in relation to this idea of consumer survival and meaningful production in their analysis and interpretation of displaced women's lives. After tracing the very arduous and physically and culturally violent conditions of the lives of these women, they go onto complicate this picture with the advancing strategies of women, which may in part have caused some of the renewed energies of patriarchal and national oppression. In their concluding section they say:

> "There were the younger women who were clearly keen on education and not early marriage, but lacked support. It still remains to be tested though, if these few women will cross the threshold/boundaries into being fully independent on all fronts. Individual women have no identity by themselves, they are always defined/linked in relation to others who are seen as the supporting networks which are themselves relatively fragile [for e.g. the immediate family, extended family, village leaders, the religious institutions, rich families etc.]
>
> Taking a firm decision to reclaim one's self identity together with the many layers that accompany it, will be a reality only if these women are supported to look at alternatives, break the sense of isolation that has been a systematic feature central to their lives and open the spaces that would equip them with the ideological means to continue their struggles. (29)

Zackariya and Ismail clearly hold onto women's self-contained subjectivity as a given and a desirable form, where it will be liberated from the constraining features of ethnicity and oppressive social conditions. They hold onto the values of the international, and international feminism as the liberating truth of identity. According to them, the women perform this need and truth in their struggles. And yet simultaneously, the women actors, displaced as they are, express an "ardent wish to go back to their traditional areas. . . . They feel that earlier they may have been poor but there was land for every family and their basic needs were met in a self-reliant way. Their struggle for political rights has to be pursued as part of resolving the ethnic conflict and women and men should be equal partners in this" (31). The study demonstrates the recognition of the importance of land as symbolic and material capital; whether these women go back to their homeland or not, their lives, struggles, and their agency is part of the national crisis, the ethnic conflict and the struggle over land. Here the women perform the international within the contested field of the nation.

There is very little left of the land of the nation for these women to perform and to translate in a bid to escape history and the forces of social factors and thereby enter universality. They perform in their own and individual ways but enter the discourses of the world through a collectivity as displaced northern Sri Lankan Muslims. How they work out strategies to survive within the difficult setting of displacement is an enactment of the international today as they resist early marriage (a new imposition spurred by the condition of displacement), fight for their right to study, to work, and to question the legal and state machinery which seems to patriarchally re-introduce certain gendered measures against them. They draw upon the discourses of international feminism and of individualism and demand to be seen as individuals with their separate and diverse needs. But the conditions of the global political and cultural economy itself complicates this picture. While these women cling onto their particular ethnic and national identity, they do so only with a numbing recognition of how it is imbricated in social processes. This tension between identity and the international, and its crisis, is painful and yet at the same time powerfully feminist for me in its contradictions and conflict. It brings alive to me how important it is to hold onto a complex understanding of gender and sexual paradigms, when grappling with the dynamism of nations, international relations, and the mobility of women. The women here are in the process of forging new identities at much cost. But nevertheless, their new identities become caught in an ever spiralling of the global, always already heterosexist, which is performed acutely in the local. As Sassen may say, these women, not travelling but displaced, become visible as international actors, the "offshore proletariat" of the international social economy of conflict, travel, and displacement.

The heritages of postcoloniality do not go away materially even in performance. The forces of class, gender, and ethnicity are pivotal in the production of the postcolonial formation as she travels through and over land. The heterosexist matrix Butler talks of here, is unavoidably performed by the uneven mapping of the world and its social forces and therefore by the mapping of the nation that shape the social culture and texture of travel.

The borderland in this sense becomes rather fraught with questions of whom it privileges. If the displaced women occupy the borders of crisis of the nation as they are marginalized many times over both in gender and in nationality, making in the process new meanings of subjectivity, they also occupy the not so easily appropriable voice of the marginal; they become silent but aggressive observers. They are quiet actors, not powerless altogether. This is the conundrum of life here. Within Sri Lanka itself this somewhat forgotten collectivity will make new meanings that could only throw into confusion the stabilities of the nation and its performances.

Hegemonically, the heritage of the postcolonial condition is the history of colonialism which is not easily dispensed with by performance and travel of the body and of the "woman." The study of place is immediate and ties in very directly with the study of hegemony. We may need to look at the heritages of woman as a place boundedness of caste, class, and sex identifications and their hegemonic implications. This may involve looking at the body as a collectivity and its deconstruction as a recognition of its history and its trajectories of action. Postcolonial feminist action in this sense is going to be fraught with these contradictions, when its bruised and bound body becomes the performance of place. The travel of gender, intra-nationally and internationally, is the containing motif of becoming women.

Women travel; they are displaced too. But these are not acts of disjuncture. The women act together as international subjects within the crises of place, nation, the international and the post-colonial today. For me this is conveyed through the attempts by Arasanayagam to make connections with women who are situated differently nationally; through Suniti Namjoshi's international travel, deconstructing and reconstructing gender beyond a sense of place; through Arundhati Roy's attempt to move outside of the nation and history; these contradictions and the impasses themselves are spelt out in the document of Zackariya and Ismail.

NOTES

1. See *The People Inbetween* by Roberts et al. for a history of the Burghers from the late 18th century until the 1960s.
2. I borrow the term "womanism" primarily from Alice Walker, who uses it as a metaphor of sustenance of an entire community. Womanism is about a woman who is also among many other things, "committed to survival and wholeness of entire people, male and female" (xi).
3. I find amazing parallels between Butler's ideas of gender performance and Namjoshi's gender enactments in *Mothers* which unfortunately cannot be gone into here.
4. Sassen's global city is in a productive dialogue with David Harvey's mapping of the modern/postmodern geography of the city within global capitalism. Harvey sees urban spatiality as a particularly capitalist phenomenon containing its contradictions of social relations in all of its acute forms. In *Consciousness and the Urban Experience*, Harvey asks for a collective politics of consumption against the hegemonic forms of capital but at the same time argues against valorizing commodity fetishism. Sassen provides an important counterpoint to what Harvey has mapped broadly and as the deep structure of an underlying and almost fixed capitalist mode of production of social relations in *Consciousness and the Urban Experience* and in *The Urbanization of Capital.* Immigrant women as

the marginalized of this urban consciousness is what Sassen sees as the transforming agency of capitalist relations and controls.

5. The Liberation Tigers of Tamil Eelam fighting for a Tamil state in the north eastern regions of Sri Lanka.

Works Cited

Arasanayagam, Jean. *Kindura: Poems by Jean Arasanyagam*. Kandy: Godamune, 1973.

———. *Reddened Water Flows Clear*. London: Forset Books, 1991.

——-. *Shooting the Floricans*. Kandy: Samjna, 1993.

———. *Trial by Terror*. Hamilton, New Zealand: Rimu Publishers, 1987.

Baudrilllard, Jean. "Simulacra and Simulations," *Selected Writings*, ed. Mark Poster. Stanford: Stanford University Press, 1988. 166-84.

Butler, Judith. *Gender Trouble: Feminism and the Subversion of Identity*. New York: Routledge, 1990.

Cohen, Jean and Andrew Arato. *Civil Society and Political Theory*. Cambridge, MA: MIT Press, 1992.

Deleuze, Gilles and Felix Guattari. *Anti-Oedipus: Capitalism and Schizophrenia*. 1977. Minneapolis: University of Minnesota Press, 1983.

de Mel, Neloufer. "Static Signifiers: Metaphors of Woman in Contemporary Sri Lankan War Poetry." *Shooting the Floricans* by Arasanayagam. ix-xvi.

Gooneratne, Yasmine. "The English Educated in Sri Lanka: An Assessment of their Cultural Role." *South Asia Bulletin* 12.1 (1992): 2-33.

Gramsci, Antonio. *Selections from Prison Notebooks*. Ed. and Trans. Quintin Hoare and G.N. Smith. New York: International Publishers, 1971.

Greenblatt, Stephen. *Renaissance Self-fashioning. From More to Shakespeare*. Chicago: Universtiy of Chicago Press, 1980.

Hall, Stuart. *The Hard Road to Renewal: Thatcherism and the Crisis of the Left*. London: Verso, 1988.

Hardt, Michael. "The Withering of Civil Society." Deleuze and Guattari, *New Mappings in Politics, Philosophy and Culture*, ed. Eleanore Kaufman and Kevin Jon Heller. Minneapolis: University of Minnesota Press, 1998. 23-39.

Harvey, David. *Consciousness and the Urban Experience: Studies in the History and Theory of Capitalist Urbanization*. Baltimore: John Hopkins University Press, 1985.

Kandiah, Thiru. "Kaduva: Power and the English Language Weapon." *Honouring E.F.C. Ludowyck*, ed. Ashley Halpe and Percy Colin Thome. Colombo: 1984. 117-54.

Lavie, Smadar, Ted Swedenburg, ed. "Introduction." *Displacement, Diaspora, and Geographies of Identity*. Durham: Duke University Press, 1996. 1-25.

Lefevbre, Henri. 1974. *The Production of Space*. Trans. Donald Nicholson-Smith. Oxford: Blackwell, 1991.

More, Thomas. 1516. *Utopia*, ed. Gerorge M. Logan and Robert M. Adams. Cambridge: Cambridge University Press, 1989.

Namjoshi, Suniti. *The Mothers of Maya Diip*. London: Women's Press, 1989.

Rajan, Gita. (Con)figuring Identity: Cultural Space of the Indo-British Border Intellectual." *Writing New Identities: Gender, Nation and Immigration in Contemporary Europe*, ed. Gisela Brinker-Gabler and Sidonie Smith. 78-99

Roberts, Michael, Ismeth Raheem and Percy Colin-Thome. *People In-between: The Burghers and the Middle Class in the Transformations within Sri Lanka, 1790s-1960s*. Vol. 1. Ratmalana, Sri Lanka: Sarvodaya, 1989.

Roy, Arundhati. *The God of Small Things*. New York: Random House, 1997.

Sassen, Saskia. *Globalization and its Discontents*. New York: The New Press, 1998.

Soja, Edward. *Postmodern Geographies: The Reassertion of Space in Critical Social Theory*. Verso, 1989.

Walker, Alice. *In Search of Our Mothers' Gardens*. San Diego: Harcourt Brace Jovanovich, 1967.

Zackariya, Faizun and Zulfika Ismail. "Early Marriage and Perpetuation of the Cycle of Violence in a Displaced Situation." Unpublished Manuscript. Colombo: 1998.

Arundhati Roy: Woman as a Writer with reference to *The God of Small Things*

ALKA SINGH
Vasanta College for Women, Varanasi

Arundhati Roy's maiden novel *The God of Small Things* is an experience and experiment of a unique kind. The pale autobiographical element emerges from a reflection of her own childhood in Ayemenam, a village in central Travancore. Although life and destiny of three generations of Syrian Christian family is depicted but on the whole it is rooted in the specific culture, society and politics of Kerala. Roy confesses in an interview to Alix Wibur, "For me the book is not about what happened, but about how what happened affected people."[1] Expanding her experiences she has dealt with the basic issues of life and fundamental universal problems faced by women. She has deftly articulated the eternal 'silence and made a courageous attack upon the conventions of the day demanding an unrestrained independence of mind for her protagonists. There is a subtle protest against the exploitation and subjugation of women. A woman's affliction mounts with the growing consciousness of her under-estimation as an article of pleasure and subservience in the masculine world. In dealing with the renaissance and resurgence of women against the existent order to preserve and develop her individuality, Roy has re-asserted her continuity with the women of the past. She has raised delicate problems and touched upon them with unusual wisdom and sanity.

Acute awareness of her role as a feminist operating in a post-colonial situation enables her to fashion her artistic strategy. She exhibits a well-defined feminist sensibility in the choice of her fictional material. The three focal points around which the novel moves is the caste question, environmental pollution and gender issue. Roy's environmental concerns endorse her affinity towards a simple and uncorrupted life. The novel is a vivid description of the personal and the socio-political cultural—neither pure fiction nor pure that, father a combination of the two. Roy herself says, 'Writing [the novel] was a fictional way of making sense of the world I lived in, and the novel, was the technical key with which I did it."[2]

Another significant feature of her debut novel is an entirely new and original technique. She appropriated the English language by bringing it under the influence of the vernacular as a device to destroy the power structure, colonial and patriarchal. She has made use of many untranslated words in order to include a truth of culture into the text. Malyalam words are embedded too in the English text. Another important characteristic is the apt use of similes and metaphors. She has beautifully exploited linguistic and rhetorical devices in the very opening of the novel so that it can be read on several levels. Another artistic treatment is that the novel begins with abundance and ends with loss. Curious spelling, capitalization, backward writing and yielding a number of Indian words to the English dictionary fall to her credit. Roy being a student of architecture earlier has employed its basics in the writing of the novel too. More or less the major part of the story is to be found in the very first chapter and thereafter the prose shutles back and forth. In one of her interviews she says: "I never believed that there was any sort of direct link between studying architecture and building buildings. So far as I am concerned, I still practise architecture. Constructing my book was actually an architectural thing."[3]

The God of Small Things makes an attack on the patriarchal notions of Kerala's touchable society; the high caste Syrian Christians and the high caste Hindus. The problems of patriarchal domination and female subalternity are rooted in the geocultural reality of Ayemenam. The male chauvinist and wife beater Pappachi who is the oldest character in the novel has a difficult time coping up with his retirement. He could not help his wife in her Pickle business for it was not dignified for an ex-Govertunent official. His frustration turns into jealousy towards his "exceptionally talented"[4] enterprising wife. He just could not appreciate her efficient management and is suspicious of the emerging woman finding a voice and vocation for herself. It is because of his insistence that "college education was unnecessary expense for a girl, his daughter Ammu had no choice but to leave Delhi and move with them" (38). Chacko, his son, the self-proclaimed Marxist is "just a case of spoiled, princeling, playing Comrade! Comrade! An Oxford Avatar of the old Zamindar mentality-a landlord forcing his attention on women who depended on him for their livelihood" (65). He had a separate entrance built for his room so that "the objects of his 'Needs' wouldn't have to go traipsing through the house" (169). Even Com. Pillai, the next candidate for the Kottayam bye-elections is not free of male chauvinism. Major characters in the novel possess a split personality. They are quite different from what they exhibit. Pappachi, an imperial entomologist, donates money to orphanages and leprosy clinics and works hard to be acknowledged as a generous moral man but is monstrous with his wife and children. The Kathakali men described as the "most beautiful of men" (230) have a magical effect in the role-play. Roy talks of Kunti, "She too was a man, but a man grown soft and womanly, a man with breasts, from doing female parts for years" (232) and yet they unmasked themselves after the show, went home to beat their wives. Chacko's exploitation came in the form of his libertine relationship with the female workers at the factory and of having deprived his sister, Ammu, a share in the family property.

The theme of exploitation and suffering is vividly dealt with through the lives of Baby Kochamma, Mammachi, Ammu and Rahel. The efficient Mammachi, handling the entire business is reduced to insignificance by her husband and is very often the target for her husband's frustration. She suffers in silence the regular beatings, considering it to be the inevitable fate of a woman. Later it is her blindness that troubles her. Probably these patriarchal norms were internalized in her for she is quite cruel in her behaviour towards the workers and insensitive to her daughter's desires. She is cruellest when Velutha arrives before her. She turns violent when she learns of Ammu's affair with Velutha: 'Her [Mammachi's] tolerance of Men's needs as far as her son was concerned, became the fuel for her unmanageable fury at her daughter" (258) for she is thoroughly upset to visualize her daughter coupling with a filthy coolie, a paravan. She felt that Ammu has "defiled generations of breeding" (258). Yet, ironically, she has no similar visualization, when she learns about her son's affairs with the working women of the factory.

Similarly Baby Kochamma, Pappachi's sister too suffers in silence carrying the burden of unstated desires buried in the depth of her heart. At the age of eighteen she falls in love with an Irish monk father Mulligan. He was flattered by her emotion that he too found irresistible many a time. This young girl and the intrepid Jesuit would stand by the well in the midday sun quaking with unchristian passion, every Thursday on his weekly visit. Defying her family she goes to Madras and becomes a Roman Catholic, just to be close to father Mulligan. Very soon, the realization dawns that it was a futile venture and she reluctantly returns home. Nevertheless "she had managed to persuade herself over the years that her unconsummated love for father Mulligan had been entirely due to her restraint and her determination to do the right thing." (45) Arundhati Roy has voiced the status of a girl through Baby Kochamma illuminating the tyrannies of the social structure that women are gripped in. She says: "a married daughter had no position in her parents' home. As for a *divorced* daughter . . . she had no position anywhere at all. And as for a *divorced* daughter from a *love* marriage, well words could not describe Baby Kochamma's outrage. As for a *divorced* daughter from an *inter community love* marriage [she] chose to remain quiveringly silent on the subject" (45-46). Baby Kochamma is shocked to hear Ammu's involvement with Velutha. "How could she stand the smell? Haven't you noticed? They have a particular smell, these Paravans" (257). Her hypocrisy is evident for maybe the smell of an Irish monk was acceptable and justified. She is responsible in enhancing Ammu's suffering and derives pleasure out of it. Once again we see that the novelist wishes to point out that these so-called high caste women have internalized the obnoxious patriarchal norms. Despite this Baby Kochamma succeeds in evoking one's sympathy for having lost her dreams at a young age and she continues to do so even at the age of eighty-three. She is an ordinary woman with a deranged mind at this age but never forgets to make the diary entry "I love you" (297).

The unfulfilled love of Baby Kochamma rendered her heartless in her treatment of Ammu. She resents Ammu for she saw her quarrelling with fate that Baby Kochamma had graciously accepted. Ammu is the worst sufferer in the novel having been deprived of education and imprisoned in Ayemenem. She gets married to escape this situation, only to realise that she had made a mistake. She married an alcoholic who beat her everyday and acted as a pimp for his boss. She aggravates him in refusing to succumb to the desire of Mr. Hollicks and thereafter divorces him to return to her house in Ayemenem—unwelcomed. But her actual agony lay in transgressing the law which ironically others had transgressed too but it was overlooked. The forbidden territory had been crossed by all and the love laws had been tampered. "The laws that lay down who should be loved, and how. And how much" (33). The violation turned out to be fatal for Ammu and her 'untouchable' lover. Velutha's technical expertise and newly-acquired religious status as a converted Christian could not serve as a substitute or grant him immunization from being a victim in a casteist society.

Ammu defies the androcentric notion and emerges as a rebel for she is a symbol of everything that men disapprove of. She avoids a surname for neither the maiden name nor her husbands name gives the "woman much of a choice" (37). In challenging the norms assigned to a woman in the patriarchal frame of reference, Ammu attempts to reclaim her body and her desires. To assert this autonomy over her body very clearly points out the feminist agenda of the novelist. Ammu refuses to conform to the rules of 'motherhood' and 'divorceehood' while Velutha, the untouchable refuses to crawl back like his ancestors. In contrast to his brother, Kuttapen was a safe, uneducated Paravan. But there exists a similarity in the destiny of the two brothers. Kuttapen fell in his attempt to pluck fruit from a coconut tree and was paralyzed while Velutha was paralyzed and killed in police custody while climbing the heights of sensual pleasure and tasting the forbidden fruit. The difference is one waited for death without reaching the fruit while the other reached it, tasted it and died. Ammu too pays for her sin as the church refuses to bury her in the end and so she is reduced to a receipt number in an electric crematorium.

Estha and Rahel, the twins, devoid of a surname, an identity, go through various emotional crisis in their futile search of a father figure. Probably they paid for their parents' sins. The unpleasant, gruesome death of Velutha and the nauseating experience of Estha at the Talkies by the Orangedrink, Lemondrink man contributes further to their insecurity and suffering. But the two share a special relationship: "He and She. We and Us" (237). They too broke the social laws of love by succumbing to the instinctual laws. Rahel shared the bed with Estha, equally an untouchable being her brother, just like their mother but the contrast is that Animu experiences ethereal joy with Velutha while Rahel and Estha had experienced "not happiness but hideous grief." (328)

The novel begins with Rahel's return from her divorced husband to see her brother/lover, Estha, to soon break the love laws while it ends with Ammu returning from her lover at the Meenachal river, with the promise to come again 'Naaley,' i.e., tomorrow. However, they never meet again for they get killed by social tyranny. The novel is definitely an insider's view of Kerala society portraying the ordinary things in an unusual way. Roy succeeds in unveiling the repulsive reality enveloped in a mask of respectability. She has dared to voice the eternal 'silence,' the 'suffering' to mark the beginning of a transformation, a revolt, an awakening.

NOTES

1. Alix Wibur, "interview," *The Week (*October 26, 1997), p. 46.
2. Praveen Swami, "Interview," *Frontline (*August 8, 1997), pp. 106-7.
3. *First City*, Delhi City Magazine, June 1997, p. 25.
4. Arundhati Roy, *The God of Small Things (*New Delhi, India Ink, 1997), p. 50.

Problematizing Issues about Home, Homeland, Diaspora and Belongingness in Transnational and National Lands: A Study of Kiran Desai's *The Inheritance of Loss*

TEJINDER KAUR
Punjabi University, Patiala

The paper aims to analyse the issues of home, homeland, diaspora and belongingness raised and problematized by Kiran Desai in her Booker Prize winning novel *The Inheritance of Loss.*[1] By setting the text in New York city of contemporary America, full of innumerable legal and illegal immigrants from many third world countries, and in Kalimpong, a small town in India at the foothills of Mount Kanchenjunga in the northeastern Himalayas which is shown passing through a political turmoil in mid-1980s in the wake of the Liberation Movement launched by the Indian-Nepalese under the banner of GNLF (Gorkha National Liberation Front), demanding Gorkhaland for the Gorkhas, who felt "constitutionally tortured" (126) and cheated by the political leaders in April 1947, now claiming their right on the land of West Bengal as their homeland because of getting "fed up with being treated like the minority in a place where they were the majority," (9) Desai has portrayed the state of homelessness, displacement, exile, marginalization and lack of belongingness being experienced by the illegal and legal diaspora communities and individuals in America (transnational land) as well as by the people from other states, regions and communities from India residing in Kalimpong (national land). In order to delineate the travails of diaspora people and communities "uprooted from their homeland" in transnational as well as national lands, Desai "deftly shuttles between first and third worlds, illuminating the pain of exile, the ambiguities of post-colonialism and the blinding desire for a better life" (blurb). By employing the technique of multiple voices (and leaving gaps and silences for the readers to fill them) to portray the complex experiences of characters in various situations both in the United States and India, Desai problematizes the issues of home, home-land, diaspora and belongingness treating them not as the fixed but as fluid concepts ever shifting with the changing positionality of the subject positions of individuals and communities in other cultures and communities with the changes in the historico-political scenarios both in home(s) and abroad.

Since the Post Second World War period, 'diaspora' as an expression and experience has expanded its terms, conditions and ramifications beyond imagination. It now signifies all migrations, settlements, journeys and movements—"voluntary or forcible"—of people and communities "from their homelands into new regions"[2] across the world, both from the Third to the First World and vice-versa, from North to South and East to West, and even from one state to another within the same nation and much more. Moreover, after the economic and political shifts following the new economic order and polarizations across continents, and since the spread of the recent phenomenon of globalization practically to all societies and nation states, diaspora experience has assumed newer and vibrant dimensions. The experience of migrancy and diaspora also engenders various problems and facets of journey and relocation in new lands e.g. displacement, uprootedness, unbelongingness, discrimination, marginalization, crisis in identity, cultural conflicts, yearning for home and homeland etc. One distinct feature of diaspora people is that in physical and material space, they live in one country but in imagination look across time and space to another and "acknowledge that the old country—a nation often buried deep in language, religion, custom or folklore—always has some claim on their loyalty and emotions," remarks Robert Cohen.[3] Thus migrants, according to Rushdie, "straddle two cultures . . .

fall between two stools."[4] The tensions and ambivalences with which diasporic consciousness is marked have been aptly enlisted by Swaraj Raj: "curious accretion of a homing desire and a state of homelessness; a state of belonging and the awareness of not being able to belong; the contradictory pulls of the nostalgic longing for the home left behind and the desire to feel at home in the new dwelling; and the discrepant centrifugal pull of staying at the margins of the centre to maintain cultural difference and the centripetal seductions of assimilations in the adopted culture."[5]

In diasporic imagination 'home' remains "a mythic place of origin and of radical lack" and as Avtar Brah states: "The concept of diaspora places the discourse of 'home' and 'dispersion' in creative tension, inscribing a homing desire while simultaneously critiquing discourses of fixed origins."[6] These issues and tensions have been explored and contested in most of diasporic discourses from multiple angles. Moreover, "Home has become such a scattered, damaged, precarious concept in our present travails," says Rushdie (*East, West* 1994)) as different people relate differently to this space in different locales and situations, here, elsewhere and also in imaginary spaces.

In the text in view, by giving us a peep into the psychic space of the characters and by showing us the miserable and "fugitive on the run" like existence of the illegal migrants from the third world countries because of "no papers" and living under the constant fear of deportation after the raids of the Immigration Authorities, shifting from one job and place to another like Biju "with folded home" under their arms, who left their homes and homelands because of craze and compulsions of various kinds in search of better job prospects and with a desire to create home away from home by grasping the green card by marrying even "the disabled and mentally retarded" green card holders, and the fake double lives led by the materially better-settled legalized diaspora, Kiran Desai reveals the pangs of displacement, homelessness, unbelongingness and nostalgia for home and homeland suffered by most of the diaspora in the transnational land. Commenting on this trait of diaspora existence, Mike Featherstone observes that "the difficulty of handling increasing levels of cultural complexity, and the doubts and anxieties . . . often engender the feelings of 'localism' in their hearts," and "the desire to return home, becomes an important theme" in their psyche "regardless of whether the home is real or imaginary, temporary, syncretized, or simulated, or whether it is manifest in a fascination with the sense of belonging, affiliation, and community attributed to the homes of others."[7]

Referring to the concept of "home-ness" in diaspora psyche, Vijay Mishra remarks that diasporas connect themselves with the ideas of home and the homeland or '*desh*' against which other lands are foreign or '*videsh*' and carry their homelands in the form of a series of objects and fragments of narratives and memories in their heads or in their suitcases, and struggle hard to preserve them in other lands and cultures.[8] Some of the Indian migrant characters in the text are shown creating 'home' in their living and psychic space with religious "icons" such as "a chunky Ganesh brought all the way from home despite its weight, for decoration plus luck in money and exams" (49) and some Muslims are portrayed preserving nicely jacketed Qurans and cuckoo clock watches waking them in the morning with the kalma of "Allah hoooo Akbar." While living on the new lands of relocations, the hatreds and prejudices for other communities and religions nurtured in their homelands too remain a part of the complex formation of their psyche. Some of them want to visit their homeland, meet their relatives, take rest and return with fresh memories, but some of them especially the illegals are not able to return. They die on the alien land only with the old photographs of families and fading memories of home and parents lurking in their minds. For some of them like Mr. Kakkar, the owner of an Indian restaurant and a travel agent, 'home' is not "a mythical place of desire" using Avtar Brah's phrase (192). Moreover, his father, living in India, has been asking him to "stay away," "not to come back to India," "a shitty place." Kakkar even advises Biju not to go back to India permanently but return to America after a short while as there is no future in India and the relatives would be expecting more money from him or he would be either robbed or hijacked. Hinting at the increasing neo-colonialism of America, he warns Biju saying that America is in the process of buying the whole world and is not going to spare people even in their homelands as they would have to work there also for one or the other American company which would pay them less there as compared to their working for these companies in America. So going by the pragmatic needs and for the better education and future of children, there is no fun in getting touchy about the home and home-country.

Some of them like Saeed Saeed from Zanzibar, Biju's fellow illegal co-worker in a bakery, though outwardly do not lament or feel the pangs of the loss of the homeland and adapt themselves very well to the requirements of the American system but in their heart of hearts, they are very rigid about the religious identity of their clan and community and also nourish and confess a feeling of hatred and revenge for the land of adoption. Some of them, more sensitive like Biju, unable to cope with the existential miseries of America, refuse to lead fake versions of life and on feeling homesick and concerned about their filial responsibility return home with a dream and desire to lead a peaceful and comfortable life with the money saved, but their "displaced homeward journey," using Stuart Hall's words,[9] proves very hazardous for them when their own homeland is shown passing through a turmoil and their parents themselves are feeling displaced in their own country as is presented happening in Kalimpong in India and through the fate met by Biju and his father. Through the portrayal of the character of London-educated anglophile judge Jemubhai Patel, Desai projects a type of immigrant returned to his homeland who though always felt uncomfortable on being treated like an outsider in Liverpool where he had gone to study for five years during the colonial regime but he never missed his home and homeland there. On his return and comfortable settlement in his homeland, he always kept himself aloof, preferred to live in English style and remained a foreigner in his own home.

Thus we find that Desai foregrounds the idea of home not as a fixed but as in transition and ambivalent location by portraying different migrants relating differently to the concepts of home, homeland and the lands of adoption as per their situations, settlements and attitudes. But in the text through the multiple experiences and situations located in India, Desai has also shown that the diasporic experience is linked not only with the transnational land, across political borders, rather it is more a matter of what JanMohammad calls, "the positionality of the subject"[10] during the historico- political clashes of power politics between communities and races. Or as Avtar Brah avers, the "power position" assumed or granted to the subject can be within the national boundaries too, and with whose shifts the categories of diasporas too change. In the parallel scenario created in the text in the post-independent India in Kalimpong in mid-1980s, Desai has revealed how in the wake of the activities of GNLF's demand for Gorkhaland, the homes of the people belonging to other states of India and especially from West Bengal and Bihar, who are considered outsiders here, are being raided and ransacked by the police and GNLF activists. The big orchard belonging to the two Bengali sisters Noni and Lola is illegally encroached and when Lola goes to complain to the village Pradhan, who is a Gorkha activist, against this act, she is insulted with lewd remarks and after coming back to her home she laments and cries over the decision of her dead husband Joydeep who had sold his entire property in Calcutta to build a home here "with such false ideas of retirement, sweet peas and mist, cat and books" where now she does not have any respect. Father Booty, a Swiss man, who has been living in Kalimpong for the past forty five years, has constructed his home here naming it "Sukhtara Star of Happiness," has established a dairy and has helped in the development of dairy system in nearby villages, too is ordered to leave immediately for his country, when he is found by the police living illegally without his papers, but who actually never felt the need to apply for papers as he always considered this place his home. He feels the pain of exile, cries bitterly while leaving his cows and buffaloes, his place, his home and his friends. Even Biju's father, who is an Indian from Uttar Pradesh and has lived half of his life in Kalimpong, also starts feeling displaced and realizes that "where he had existed in what seemed a sweetness of crabbiness—was showing him now that he had been wrong. He wasn't wanted in Kalimpong and he didn't belong" (278) when during the protest rally of GNLF, violence breaks out and non-Nepalis are being chased to be killed. In this atmosphere, Nepalis, who earlier used to feel like diaspora on being side-tracked and treated like slaves on the land of their ancestors, have now risen to the subject position. They start looting, hating, ignoring and passing sultry remarks at all the outsiders who had left their homes in the other states and regions of India to settle here and live a luxurious life at their cost. They now force them to feel diasporic (especially the Bengalis and Biharis). How communities shift their stands during the situations of power struggle is shown through the recent joining of Tibetans, Lepchas and Sikkimese with the Nepalis in this hate wave to be on the safe side, whereas earlier they used to project themselves different from Nepalis considering them inferior.

Thus we see that the text of the novel through many situations, experiences and ambivalent stands of different characters highlights the "tense," "chaotic," "antagonistic" and "shifting" locations of the diaspora both in the lands of the first and third worlds. The subtext of the novel further problematizes and raises more issues for the consideration of the readers not only about the precarious, disgraced and displaced lives and existence, shifting positions and identities of the diasporas but also about the concepts of home, homeland and belongingness in the changing historico-political and existential situations both in home(s) and abroad .

If "home" is a place" where we gather grace" as Nissim Ezekiel says in his poem "Enterprise" then where are the homes of Lola, Noni, Mrs. Sen and of others which they had built in Kalimpong and where they are now being disgraced?

If violence, arson and insult leashed by the Gorkhas on the non-Nepalis in their demand for their own homeland seem to Lola and a few other characters in the text as unjustified and fundamentalist activities fit to be condemned in a secular country like India then how far is the hateful attitude of other people living in Kalimpong towards Nepalis justified, especially that of Lola, who always talked of we "bongs" and they "neps," "all budhoos," "no brains," "louts" and untrustworthy, who would kill you for mere fifty rupees? Desai problematizes this issue of the justification of the demand of the Gorkhas for their homeland through the speech made by the GNLF leader who projects them as "brave and loyal soldiers" always deprived of decent living and now of their fundamental rights even in their own independent country and also through Noni's voice who counters her sister's notions by arguing with her to consider the appropriateness of the struggle of Nepalis from their point of view also who since long have been displaced and thrown out by one country or the other and who certainly needed their own homeland and the opportunities to lead a dignified life and run their administration in their own language.

Is the Nepali youths' struggle for liberation and possession of their homeland motivated by their patriotic feelings or for making money only by looting the outsiders which disillusions Gyan, a Nepali Maths tutor and lover of Sai (Jemubhai Patel's granddaughter) who confesses before her his desire to leave this place (his proposed homeland) and go with her to Australia, away from history and family liabilities and make there a home, afresh?

Is there any relationship between diasporas acquiring citizenship of the adopted country and the sense of belongingness with that country, the issue which has been explored at length by May Joseph in the book *Nomadic Identities: the Performance of Citizenship*?[11] If Saeed Saeed has married a girl from a family of long-haired Vermont hippies for getting the legal status, does it ensure that he would relate to American land by heart and be loyal to it? Though he has made himself at home in America after having made a place for himself among the Americans and the outsiders, yet he calls himself first a Muslim then an American and declares that his aim in getting citizenship of America is in fact an act of revenge. Even the family he has got connected to after his marriage for getting hold of the green card gives assurance about him, welcoming him through a letter to the INS but they also clarify to Saeed that for "Any subversion against the U.S government—they would be happy to help" (123). On the other hand is the example of Father Booty who is turned out from India on the ground of his illegal stay here, who though never bothered to apply for citizenship in India but still created a real home here for himself and others around, in other words who related to India through heart.

If diaspora theorists and writers speak of the displaced, homeless and precarious existence of diasporas in the adopted lands because of their non-adoption by heart by the host country, do diasporas too not go and live there only for material gains and nurture hatred for the natives in their hearts and minds even after acquiring the citizenship of their native land? Though outwardly they pose assimilation and acculturation but inwardly they are full of the feelings of anger and revenge as is shown by Desai through the outwardly extra-polite behaviour with American customers and nightly confessions of Harish-Harry (the owner of the Gandhi Café) before Biju, who strongly desires to break the necks of these Americans or wishes his son to fulfil his dream by doing so with the sons of Americans.

If diaspora existence is termed as 'belonging nowhere' existence as diasporas suffer the pangs of in-betweenness then where do the loyalties of diaspora actually lie—to the land they have left or the one where they are earning their livelihood? Norman Tebbit raises this issue by asking two questions: "The cricket test—which side do they cheer for? . . . Are you still looking back to where you came from or where you are?"[12] Moreover, during the times of crises for the adopted countries, do the diasporas feel concerned for them, or their loyalties always remain basically with their home countries, the question which has been very pertinently raised by Jarnail Singh, a Punjabi writer, in his short story "Tower." where after the 9/11 attack when immigrants hold America responsible for this attack on World Trade Centre, an American character remarks that these legal immigrants who though call themselves Americans and boast proudly of their green cards and enjoy the rights to live comfortable lives as American citizens but in reality they always remain loyal to their countries of origin.[13] The confessions of Saeed Saeed and Harish-Harry too contest this issue of diaspora belongingness and loyalty.

If "Home is where I began, and where I shall return" signifying roots, as Sura P. Rath[14] says and if for Dorrine Kondo home "stands for a safe place, where there is no need to explain oneself to outsiders,"[15] then is Biju's unannounced and empty-handed journey back home going to be welcomed by his father, who himself is passing through a phase of imminent helplessness, and do both of them feel safe there? No doubt, Biju's heart "throbs" at the thought and sight of his native land in Walter Scott's words (in his poem "The Native Land") but does Biju's unbecoming treatment by his own countrymen who rob him naked which makes him reflect over the foolishness of his decision to come back to his home and homeland whose imaginary ideal images he had been constructing in his memories, not make the readers side with his reflections?

The questions whether thrice-displaced Biju should go back to America or he will have to go back as his twice-displaced father would neither desire nor would he be able to set a new home for him here in the prevailing scenario or they would have to return to their ancestral village land in UP, their original homeland whose peaceful and idyllic locale they used to reconstruct and miss together in Kalimpong, to start their life of struggle afresh because of abject poverty, have been left open-ended by the novelist. Will Biju's compulsion to go back not make him pass through the same degrading process of humiliation and disgraceful existence in foreign lands is also a question left before the readers to ponder over.

To sum up, it can be said that by portraying the craze and compulsions of diasporic journey across the nations and from one region to another within the nation itself which entails various travails associated with it, Desai has shown her characters leading the lives of dislocation—physical, psychological, emotional, ancestral and political—both in the alien land and homeland and has also problematized the issues about home, homeland, diaspora and belongingness by treating these from multiple angles.

Works Cited

1. Kiran Desai, *The Inheritance of Loss* (Penguin, 2006).
2. Bill Ashcroft, Gareth Griffiths and Helen Tiffin, ed. *Key Concepts in Post-Colonial Studies* (Routledge, 1998), p. 68.
3. Robert Cohen, *Global Diasporas: An Introduction* (UCI Press, 1997), p. ix.
4. Salman Rushdie, *Imaginary Homelands* (London: Granta, 1999), p. 15.
5. Swaraj Raj, "Theorizing Diaspora Poetics and Diaspora Literature," *Perspectives on Diaspora Indian Fiction in English*, ed. Tejinder Kaur and N.K. Neb (Jalandhar: Nirman, 2005), p. 17.
6. Avtar Brah, *Cartographies of Diaspora: Contesting Identities* (Routledge, 1997), pp. 192-93.
7. Mike Featherstone, "Localism, Globalism, and Cultural Identity" in *Global/ Local: Cultural Productions and the Transnational Imaginary*, ed. Rob Wilson and Wimal Dissanayake (Durham: Duke UP, 1996), p. 47.
8. Vijay Mishra, "New Lamps for Old: Diasporas Migrancy Border" from *Interrogating Post-Colonialism: Theory, Text and Context*, ed. Harish Trivedi and Meenakshi Mukherjee (1996: rpt. 2000, IIAS, Shimla), pp. 67-68.
9. Stuart Hall, "Cultural Identity and Diaspora," *Colonial Discourse and Post-Colonial Theory: A Reader*, ed. Patrick Williams and Laura Chrisma (New York: Harvester Wheatsheaf, 1994), p. 399.
10. S.X. Goudie, *Theory, Practice and the Intellectual: A Conversation with Abdul R. JanMohammed.* 10April2004. 10May2004. http: //social.chass.nscu.edu/jouvert/v/i2/Goudie.htm., p. 8.

11. (Minneapolis: University of Minnesota Press, 1999).
12. Qtd. Zadie Smith, *White Teeth* (Penguin, 2000), p. 123.
13. Jarnail Singh, *Towers (*Ludhiana: Chetna, 2005), p. 31.
14. Sura P. Rath, *Home(s) Abroad: Diasporic Identities in Third Spaces.* 10 April 2004. 10 May 2004. http://social.chass.ncsu.edu/ jouvert/ v4i3/ rathl.htm., p. 8.
15. Dorrine Kondo, "The Narrative Production of 'Home,' Community, and Political Identity in Asian American Theatre," *Displacement Diaspora, and the Geographies of Identity*, ed. Smadar Lavie and Ted Swedenberg (Durham: Duke UP, 1996), p. 97.

Predominant Issues in Kiran Desai's *The Inheritance of Loss*

F.A. INAMDAR
Aurangabad

Kiran Desai like Alexander Dumas and Martin Amis did not end up by becoming grass and fern under big trees. She sowed seeds of greatness in her maiden work *Hullabaloo in the Guava Orchard.* The very second novel won Booker prize in 2006.

In *The Inheritance of Loss*, Kiran Desai talks about human dignity and loss of it by the protagonist of the novel, Jemubhai Patel from Piphit, Gujarat. He is called by Desai "a lizard man." He is a retired judge who lives on the hillside of Kalimpong in a mountainous region of North East South India, with 'a hunchbacked cook, a lush-lashed maiden and a long-tailed wolf dog.'[1] The 'lush-lashed maiden' shows the influence of the mother, Anita Desai's character in *Fire on the Mountain* on Kiran Desai, where we have a granddaughter, Raka, and grandmother, Nanda Kaul—a recluse and emotionless woman, living a vegetable life like the retired judge Jemubhai Patel. But *The Inheritance of Loss* has a vast canvas. It encompasses issues, such as shadow class immigrants aspiring for green card in America and consequently returning to India, penniless, pitiable and demented like the cook's son, Biju and the other friends of Biju, leading a waif's life. To this issue, Kiran Desai closely connects madness of Indians for America and its cultured, civilized and materialistically most satisfying life on earth.

This problem is linked up with the disruptive and debilitating impact of postcolonialism on the psychic life and social attitudes of the resident Indians. The author is concerned with the dark side of globalisation creating a great gulf of difference between the rich and the poor. It evokes a stunning portrait of people with crumbling hopes nurtured on the Western notion of rationality and superiority of the white race; the global recession and the bursting of the American bubble. Moreover, the novelist is a powerful critique of the cotemporary socio-political situation. It has given birth to class differences, inequality, insurgence and terrorist violence, which leaves the reader paralysed to see the plight of Biju joining his father. It is a harrowing picture of how the individual lives are crushed by the terrorists and make a mess of all acceptable values.

Sai-Gyan romance is exploded as Gyan joins the insurgent Gorkhas. Sai's life is linked with history. Religious, racial, class, and gender differences give rise to the conflict in the novel.

I

Against the background of globalisation, multiculturalism, modernisation, terrorism and insurgency we have to see how Desai has evoked Jemubhai's life. His life is presented in retrospect. From the narrative he emerges as an ambitious, self-centred, cynical individual, "a detestable character" (22)[2] as Harish Sawhney calls him. He also represents the class of bureaucrats who subserve the interest of the British during the colonial rule. In his craze for excellence in colonial rule, he ill-treats his wife, ignores his relatives, indulges in the cynical exercise of power and degrades himself as a human being.

Mr. Jemubhai had left home at the age of 20, with a black tin trunk in 1939. His home, from where he had left for Liverpool to Cambridge, was Piphit in Gujarat. The novelist narrates Jemubhai's father's profession as opposed to his son's. While Jemubhai was a judge, his father was procuring false witnesses to appear in court. Ironically Jemubhai's father "was proud of his ability to influence and corrupt the path of justice, exchange right for wrong or wrong for right" (57). Such a man could not have had enough money to send his son to Cambridge to pass his ICS, but he manages to do that by choosing for his son a fabulously rich man's daughter, though a dark and ugly daughter of a rich man seemed their best bet. That rich man was Bomanbhai Patel. He was the official supplier of horse feed to the British military encampment at Pophit. This man's double standard of deceitful existence attracts the novelist's interest. She says: "He offered soldiers unauthorized women in an unauthorized part of town" (89) though he had kept his women under purdah which had increased his honour.

Immediately after one month of the wedding, Jemubhai had to leave for Cambridge. His first night with his wife is ironically described: "She was fourteen years old and he had yet to examine her face" (36). During his journey on sea in his cabin bunk, he thinks about his wife how 'he had undressed and hurriedly redressed his wife, of how he had glimpsed her expression, just bits and pieces of it in slipping of the "pallu over her head and in the memory of the closeness of the female flesh, his penis reached up in the dark and waved about' (38). After he returns from England taking his ICS degree, Jemubhai fails to lead a meaningful life. His consummation of the marriage with his wife is shown as a ridiculous and laughable affair.

It all begins with his search for his missing powder puff. In fact, his wife, Nimi, earlier called Bela, takes a fancy for that. Consequently, she unbuttons her blouse and powders her breasts. It was so attractive to her 'so foreign, so silken, she stuffed inside'. Then begins Jemubhai's search for it. He shouts at the Patel Ladies spread-eagled on mats in the veranda shade (167). The novelist builds up a hilarious incident out of this search. Jemubhai's mother asks him: "Is anything wrong with your skin?" His sister laughs and tells: "we sent you abroad to become a gentleman, and instead you have become a lady!" When the excitement spread, all the relatives from Patel clan assemble. "The kakas kakis, masas masis, phuas phois." To Jemubhai's horror, this gathering appears to be "a composite monster with multiple arms and legs that came cartwheeling in, raising the dust, screaming, hundreds of hands were held, over the monster's hundreds of giggling mouths. Who had stolen what?" (167)

The novelist reveals through this incident how very inhuman Jemubhai himself is. He is least social; a selfish and monstrous figure. Jemubhai as a detestable character who has made a mess of his life is brought out in his first union with his wife. This is the most beautiful moment of one's life. And it is turned into an episode of hatred towards his wife: "He did not like his wife's face, searched for his hatred, found beauty, dismissed it. Once it had been a terrifying beckoning thing that had made his heart turn to water. An Indian girl could never be as beautiful as an English one" (168). He notices the puff sticking out between the hooks and pulls forth, like a bursting ruined heart: 'His dandy puff' (168). She slips from his grasp and his anger flies. He comes at her with a look of murder: "He clamped down on her, tussled her to the floor, . . . in a dense frustration of lust and fury—penis uncoiling, mottled purple-black as if with rage, blundering, uncovering the chute—he stuffed his way ungracefully into her." (169)

When he takes her to Bonda, his place of posting, his sexual encounters with his wife are compared by the novelist to "The same blank look of a dog or monkey humping in the bazaar" (172).

He never speaks and looks in her direction. She was uncared for, her freedom is useless, her husband disregarded his duty. He hates her bum. He calls her lazy, wide as a buffalo. He even hates tinkle-tonk of her bangles. And orders her to remove "those trinkets off." (172) When one day he finds footprints on the toilet seat, he barely contains his outrage. He takes her head and pushes it in the bowl. These physical and mental tortures make her invalid. She begins falling asleep during day and wakes up in the middle of the night. Jemubhai's tortures create dislike to see her in the mirror because she could not see herself in it. Because of the psychological tortures of Jemubhai, her cheeks erupt. He considers her fallen beauty as a further affront. He is afraid of touching her as a result of her skin disease. To top it all, he discourages and orders her not to show her face outside lest people might run from her screaming. This is how the novelist makes Jemubhai misogynist and a degrading selfish animal. She stays in her sister's house in which she burns herself to death while cooking. The novelist sums up the brutal picture of Jemubhai: "Now Jemubhai wondered if he had killed his wife for the sake of false ideals. Stolen her dignity, shamed his family, shamed hers, turned her into the embodiment of their humiliation." (308)

As for his daughter: "He had condemned the girl to convent boarding schools. [She] relieved when she reached a new height of uselessness and absurdity by eloping with a man who had grown up in an orphanage" (308).

Jemubhai's treatment of his cook goes beyond the torture and inhumanity of his wife. It is linked up with the judge's love for the bitch which is identified with his face, forehead, nose, chin, lack of movement, lack of lips and fixed gaze: "more than a reptile in the slope of his face, the wide hairless forehead, the introverted nose, the introverted chin, his lack of movement, his lack of lips and fixed gaze" (33). Like the dog, the judge also sits at a place before his chess. The cook, the judge and the dog parallel one another. The judge as a sadist and the cook as a masochist: "The judge and his cook had lived together for more years than they had with anyone else . . . in the same room, closer to each other than to any other human being and—nothing, zero, no understanding" (33).

The sadistic attitude of the judge is revealed when the dog goes missing. The Judge cannot bear it. When the cook goes in search of the dog in the tavern—the people laugh at the news and say: "In a place where people died without being given any attention. They died of T.B., hepatitis, leprosy, plain old fever. . . . And no jobs, no work, nothing to eat . . . this commotion over dog! Ha ha, ha" (314).

When the cook fails to trace out the bitch, the judge resorts to beating the cook and the cook submits to his torture:

> He wants to kill me. Let him kill me. What is my life? . . . It is useless to you and to me. Kill me! Maybe that will give you satisfaction. Go on! (320).

After ruthlessly beating the cook, we see the judge lying "exhausted in his bed. The cook sat in the kitchen, his face still in the grip of a nightmare" (323).

II

The cook's illusion about his son's earning money and making glamorous life evokes the plight of immigrants. Many Indians get into the USA illegally and lead a waif's life. At home, the parents boast of their children leading a life cushioned in luxury, whereas their children lead a gutter life amidst mice crawling on their bodies.

The novelist depicts such a life of illusion and reality in the life of the cook and his son, Biju. After chasing and changing jobs after jobs Biju is finally frustrated, and decides to return to India. His journey back home is so pathetic and horrific that anyone reading about it would prefer to starve in his own country than venture into greener pastures. Against this background we have to see how Biju's mindset does not desist from going home in spite of the fact that the proprietor of the newly opened Shangri-la Travel, Mr. Kakkar, reminds Biju of his (i.e. Kakkar's) father's advice to him:

> My father, so long as he was alive, he always told me, "Good, stay away, don't come back to this shitty place" (269).

Mr. Kakkar warns Biju that once he is back in India every one will ask for dollars from Biju, as if "you shit and dollars come out. If they won't the robbers will." He adds further: "Some disease will; if not some disease, the heat will; if not the heat, those mad Sardarjis will bring down your plane before you even arrive" (269).

Biju, like his father, the cook, is a man filled with illusions. After he goes back to India, he dreams: "he would buy a taxi. His savings were small, collected in his shoe, his sock, his underwear, through all these years, but he thought he could manage it. He would drive up and down the mountain side on market days, gold tinsel, gods above the dash-board, a comical horn, Pawpum Pom paw. . . . And he'd build a house with solid walls, a roof that would not fly off every monsoon season." (286)

The most pitiable and emotional illusion conjured up by Biju is: "Biju played the scene of meeting his father again like a movie in his head, wept a bit at the thought of so much happiness and emotion" (286).

I am really moved by the remarkable ability of the novelist for the emotional scene conjured up above. Everyone of us has gone through such moments in life and Kiran Desai will be remembered for her ability to create such emotions.

Kiran Desai evokes the craze of expatriates buying foreign made goods while returning home. This is shown through Biju's buying spree:

> Biju went to Jackson Heights . . . he bought a TV and VCR, a camera, sunglasses, baseball caps that said "NYC" and "Yankees" and "I like My Beer Cold and Women Hot," a digital two-time clock and radio and cassette player, waterproof watches, calculators, electric razor, a toaster oven, winter coat, nylon sweaters, polyester cotton shirts, a polyurethane quilt, a rain jacket, a folding umbrella, suede shoes, a leather wallet, a Japanese-made heater, a set of sharp knives, a hot-water bottle, fixodent, saffron, cashews and, raisins, aftershave, T-shirts with "I love NY" and "Born in the USA" . . . a bottle of perfume called windsong . . . who was that for? He didn't yet know her face. (270)

The long quotation lists illusion, vanity and the foolish craze to show that one is foreign-returned and has to be held in high esteem. Thus, these are things bought by an idiot full of sound and fury signifying nothing. And we are all whoring after English gods, and dream of being born in New York and love New York. Kiran Desai calls us all 'English bastards.'

Ultimately what happens to Biju happens to all of us in a country torn off by insurgency: They denude him of the things he had brought, including his wallet, shoes, belt, jeans and Tshirt. He is made to stand in his white underpants. The most pathetic thing is:

> He ran into the jungle chased by the dogs. . . . Darkness fell and he sat right in the middle path—without his baggage, without his savings, without his pride. Back from America with far less than he'd ever had (317).

Kiran Desai symbolically exhibits that Biju's denuding is purging of his dreams and illusions of America and its greatness and facing stark reality of the Indian existence. His illusion is "heard no more" and he joins his father, the cook with his bare self:

> "Pitaji?" said the figure, all ruffles and colours. . . . "Biju?" Whispered the cook. "Biju!" he yelled, demented." (324)

Biju and the like do not make hay in America. They are exploited by the employer as Biju puts it to Harish-Harry: "This is how you make your money, paying us nothing because you know we can't do anything, making us work day and night because we are illegal. Why don't you sponsor us for our green cards?" (188)

Harish-Harry spells American dream for the Indians. Every one in America is after earning money at the cost of spiritual, ethical and moral considerations: "Another day another dollar, penny saved is penny earned, no pain no gain, business is business, gotta do what ya gotta do" (149). For earning money, Biju sleeps in places infested with rats. This, he realizes, in Harish Harry's Gandhi Cafe: "The rats of his earlier jobs had not forsaken Biju. They were here, too, exulting in the garbage, clawing through wood, making holes that Harish-Harry stuffed with steel wool and covered with bricks. . . . One chewed Biju's hair at night." (147)

This is ironically contrasted by Kiran Desai by evoking the cook's illusion about his son's life in America. The novelist calls him only the cook. Symbolically he has no status, no individuality like the Africans in Conrad's *Heart of Darkness*. "My son works in New York," the cook boasted to everyone he met. "He is a manager of a restaurant business" (84). The cook has the foolish audacity to tell the doctor: "My son has a new job in USA" (85). This picture is observed in Biju: "the homeless man often slept in a dense chamber of green that seemed to grow not so much from soil as from a fertile city crud. A homeless chicken also lived in the park. Every now and then Biju saw it scratching in a homey manner in the dirt and felt a pang for village life" (81). It is needless to say that the man and the chicken express the pitiable predicament of Biju in Hell called the USA.

At Freddy's, Biju accepts the job of delivery of food to various customers. He pounds at the pedals:

> a tremulous figure between heaving buses, regurgitating, taxis. . . . They harassed Biju with such blows from their horns as could split the world into whey and solids: Paaa Awww! (49)

During the cold season "Once, on his bicycle, he began to weep from the cold, and the weeping unpicked a deeper vein of grief—such a terrible groan issued from between the whimpers that he was shocked his sadness was so profound" (51).

This image contrasts with the cook's illusion of Biju's life back home in India: "He imagined sofa TV bank account. Eventually Biju would make enough and the cook would retire. He would receive a daughter-in-law to serve him food, crick-crack his toes, grandchildren to swat like flies." (17)

As a parallel to Biju's life in the USA, Kiran Desai depicts the life of Jemubhai in Cambridge: Jemubhai suffers from isolation. He grows 'stranger to himself' (40). He develops schizophrenic tendencies: "found his own skin odd-coloured, his own accent peculiar. He forgot how to laugh . . . he held his hand over his mouth, because he could not bear anyone to see his gums, his teeth . . . would prefer shadow to light, . . . he was suspicious that sunlight might reveal him." (40)

I have laid a great stress on the plight of the immigrants going abroad either for their livelihood or for getting degrees. Biju and Jemubhai Popatlal are ruined—one having urge to earn dollars, and the other, though educated, falls a prey to the spurious ideal of the white race, and consequently ruins his family life and status. Instead of being a good human being by not submitting to his false pride, and by bringing up his granddaughter with loving care and by treating his cook as a human being and consequently, earning love, dignity and fellowship, he would have possessed the cultural inheritance, and could have attained happiness in his life. The image of insurgency is an eye opener to see human beings as beasts of prey. This is the loss of inheritance. Moreover, Kiran Desai has brought out the caste hatred through Mrs. Sen's views which form a central pillar of Hindu belief. Her views go like this: "So strict was the Koran that its teachings were beyond human capability. Therefore Muslims were forced to pretend one thing, do another, they drank, smoked, ate pork, visited prostitutes, and then denied it" (130).

Such a view about Muslims is biased and partial. With all such vision, Kiran Desai's views of India appear to be of Lola: "She thought of India as a concept, a hope, or a desire" (238). Like John Steinbeck's view in his Nobel acceptance speech that the writer celebrates "man's capacity for greatness . . . for courage, compassion and love," Kiran Desai not only presents in this novel bleak immigrant realities but also celebrates the union of the father and the son, the lover and the beloved, the bitch and the judge.

Despair is created when Biju comes back to his father but only his desire exists. Here Godot appears broken down but the cook's desire exists as an eternal mirage. This appears to be the thematic nexus of the novel: "The peaks of Kanchenjunga turned golden with the kind of luminous light." (324) The imagery of light as opposed to the pitch darkness from where Biju escaped followed by the dogs amply evokes the central vision of the novel.

NOTES

1. Kiran Desai, *The Inheritance of Loss* (New Delhi: Penguin, 2006).
2. Sawhney, Harish. "In the Wide World." Rev. of *The Inheritance of Loss. The Times Literary Supplement*, 22 Sept. 2006.

Aravind Adiga's *The White Tiger*: A Critical Response

PRATIBHA NAGPAL
Punjab University

Published in 2008, *The White Tiger* by Aravind Adiga has generated tremendous response both from the literary and academic circle. Critics have been equally lavish in praising the book as they have been in condemning it. Hailed as extraordinary and brilliant, thrilling and insightful, witty and unpretentious, the novel is considered as one of the most powerful books published in decades by some. Critics have also opined that the novel is tedious and unfunny, disappointing and absurd, patronizing and officious, reading more like the thriller magazines without any moral purpose or justification. Pertinent here to point out about *The White Tiger* is:

> (A)s a debut, it marks the arrival of a storyteller who strikes a fine balance between the sociology of the wretched place he has chosen as home and the twisted humanism of the outcast. With detached, scatological precision, he surveys the grey remoteness of an India where the dispossessed and the privileged are not steeped in the stereotypes of struggle and domination. The ruthlessness of power and survival assumes a million moral ambiguities in this novel. (S. Prasannarajan, *India Today)*

The purpose of this paper is to review *The White Tiger* as a novel of Black Comedy and a novel that focuses on the binary nature of a nation marching towards its tryst with destiny. As a genre, Black Comedy is marked by an invincible sense of disillusionment and cynicism, with little or no hope of escape or change available to the protagonists. A sense of fatalism pervades the text, in which the protagonists choose sardonic humor as a means of expressing themselves because they cannot do anything about their fate or circumstances. According to screen writer John Truby,

> When black comedy is used as a basis for a story's plotline, it involves a society in an unhealthy state and a main character wanting something which, for whatever reason, is not a thing that will be beneficial to himself or society. The audience should usually be able to see this for themselves, and often a supporting character within the story also sees the insanity of the situation. The main character rarely if ever learns a lesson or undergoes any significant change from the ordeal. http://en.wikipedia.org/wiki/ black_ comedy

If one were to view *The White Tiger* in light of the above statement, it would become clear that Adiga has indeed used this genre to challenge the fascinating journey of the nation towards development and to punch a hole in the collective euphoria of India's middle class and its policy makers. Step by step, Adiga bares the startling reality of a nation where unplanned, haphazard urbanization and colonization is suffocating the already overburdened infrastructure, where the social fabric is being stretched to a breaking point, where poverty, corruption, disease, moral degeneration still rule the day and where every known tradition is being put to test.

The White Tiger is presented in the form of epistolary novel, a series of letters written over a period of seven nights, in which, the protagonist Balram, narrates his rags to riches story to the premier of China, Wen Jiabao, who is to visit Bangalore, India's Information Technology capital. These letters become the confessional mode through which the narrator tells of how he became a successful entrepreneur and his journey from a small non-descript village Laxmangarh to Bangalore. Within this story is contained the perspective of the one who exists on the periphery and his responses to each and every situation that he encounters in modern India. Born to a rickshaw-puller, living in the small village of Laxmangarh, the protagonist does not even have a name that he can call his own and is named Balram by his teacher the day he is sent to school. It is a village that represents "at least a third of the country, a fertile place, full of rice fields and wheat fields and ponds." (14) But those who live in this village call it the "Darkness." Adiga makes it very clear in the beginning of the novel "that India is two countries in one: an India of Light, and an India of Darkness" (14). Balram is extraordinarily responsive to the world around him and through his observations the reader gets to know the two Indias. While his village is showcased as the model of the amenities that are provided by the government in its plans, the reality is that everything in the village is defunct and broken. Its people are malnourished and lead a life of utter misery and poverty, leading a day-to-day existence without any hope for a better future. The landlord family who control the village, its land and people are rightly called "The Buffalo," " The Stork," "The Wild Boar," "The Raven" by Balram, according to the characteristics that they show. Together they form a mafia that controls everything—the river, the agricultural land, the roads, and the hillside. Not content to stay in such demeaning conditions, Balram slowly manages to distance himself from his family and to go to the city to get a driving license and look for his opportunity, which comes to him eventually when he gets a job as a driver with the son of his landlord "The Stork," Mr. Ashok and his wife Pinky. His job as a driver opens up new avenues for his ever-inquisitive mind and the reader is informed in great detail about the haves and have-nots in India and the manner in which the people employed as domestic help are treated. A quick learner, Balram keeps his eyes and ears open for any information or snatches of conversation that he can gather. It takes him no time to realize that hierarchy, sycophancy, corruption and ruthlessness is the rule of the day. It appears as if India is like a vast jungle where whosoever can, bullies and exploits the one weaker than him.

With unflinching brutality Adiga describes how the servants bully and blackmail each other for petty thefts and benefits; how landlords are made to pay hefty sums as bribes to politicians in order to carry on with their illegal business; how teachers are clueless about child psychology and steal money meant for the meals to be served to the students in the schools, under the Government policy; how uniforms are stolen and sold out by teachers who have not been paid wages by the Government. In Delhi, Balram is a witness to his employer, Mr. Ashok, paying bribes to politicians and taking their assistant to shady hotels being run openly, and the flesh trade being carried on brazenly. Even the Great Socialist who contests and wins from Laxmangarh is nothing better than a wheeler dealer who is a party to the scam of the landlords taking coal for free from the Government mines in return for the bribes paid to him on regular basis. Once in the city, Balram realizes that there are two Indias: one which shines bright with multistoried buildings, big Malls, air conditioned cars, IT savvy people, call centres and the other, of the ones who work for and attend on those, a part of the Shining India. In this India, fatal accidents caused by drunken owners of the big cars are not reported, the police is bribed to keep everything under wraps and if need be, drivers are made to sign confessionals in advance to safeguard the master of the cars; traffic jams are combatted with air conditioned cars; and money exchanges hands frequently for getting things done. As the novel progresses, Balram becomes a witness to the glitz as well as the unjust system around him and begins to question his position as a servant, his place in society which leads to his resenting his conditioning for such a life. He begins to long for a better life for himself and is no longer proud to wear the driver's uniform, which in the beginning of the novel had so fascinated him. He wants to wear good clean clothes, go to places his master and mistress visit and in short he begins desiring the basic things of life which have so far been denied to him by circumstances, the system and his own passive acceptance of his condition.

The murder of his master Ashok is his way of getting social justice and in somewhat a predictable manner Balram moves very fast to reach Bangalore through a crisscross journey, along with his nephew, whom he has avowed to give a better life than his own. Once in Bangalore Balram soon establishes himself as a successful entrepreneur, with the seven lakh rupees that he has stolen from his master after killing him. He now calls himself Ashok Sharma, and is the proud owner of sixteen SUVs which he uses as taxis and has drivers working for him. He is kind to his "boys" and treats them like "family" and not servants and has a fair, dignified employer-employee relationship with them, taking care of their needs and any mishap that may befall them in the course of their duty. Throughout the novel Adiga maintains a sardonic tone and the reader does not get any insight into why things happen as they do or if there is any way out of the gory situation in which the protagonist finds himself. Balram's cockiness at times appears shocking to the reader especially in parts where he mocks at the number of Gods that he can pray to and where he confesses to the murder and boasts of his achievements as an entrepreneur. It is equally difficult to understand the disrespect that he shows to Mahatma Gandhi and the scornful and sardonic tone of the narrator sets the novel as black comedy but lessens any sympathy one could have for the protagonist who is indeed right in narrating the world around him in a fairly true tone. Adiga uses the image of the Rooster Coop to describe the Indian scenario. Balram, deliberating over the fact that in India millions of people are involved in various jobs ranging from delivering furniture and carrying back cash payment in thousands for the master; driving cars and seeing or handling a lot of money, sometimes in millions, for their masters; carrying suitcases full of cut diamonds for their masters. And the people engaged in these jobs as servants never think of running away with the money or the merchandise, which may be worth their year or two years of salary or perhaps a steal which could last them throughout their miserable lives. The reason why this is so because 99.9% of people are caught in a Rooster Coop situation:

> Go to Delhi, behind Jama Masjid, and look at the way they keep chicken there in the market. Hundreds of pale hens and brightly coloured roosters, stuffed tightly into wire-mesh cages, packed as tightly as worms in a belly, pecking each other and shitting on each other, jostling just for breathing space; the whole cage giving off a

> horrible stench—the stench of terrified, feathered flesh. On the wooden desk above this coop sits a grinning young butcher, showing off the flesh and organs of a recently chopped-up chicken, still oleaginous with a coating of dark blood. The roosters in the coop smell the blood from above. They see the organs of their brothers lying around them. They know they're next. Yet they do not rebel. They do not try to get out of the coop.
>
> The very same thing is done with human beings in this country. (173-74)

Sarcastically Adiga takes away the last vestibule of dignity- their honesty, from these sad people existing on the periphery and attributes their situation to their conditioning. They "exist in perpetual servitude; a servitude so strong that you put the key of his emancipation in a man's hand and he will throw it back at you with a curse." (176) Towards the end of the novel when Balram proclaims that he has broken free of this rooster coop situation, the reader already knows that it is not on account of a moral vision or growth but due to the twist of the writer's cynical tone in the novel. *The White Tiger* abounds in instances of pessimistic, gloomy and derisory humour which negates the lives of people like Balram and there appears to be no meaning in their existence except that they live in The Great Indian Rooster Coop.

All established norms of family, moral values, tradition and belief are mocked at or treated with disdain by Balram. River Ganga is the black river—the river of death; people start prayers by "kissing some god's arse" and there are 36,000,004 gods for the Hindus; democracy is mocked at; mobile phones "corrode a man's brain, shrink his balls and dry up his semen" (38); Mahatma Gandhi is scoffed at for his honesty and dedication; people change religion to get petty jobs and fall victims to blackmail by fellowmen; prostitution, debauchery, deceit and falsehood are the accepted norm of life and anything goes in the name of power and corruption. In fact Balram gives a whole new definition to the great spirit of Indian democracy and rewrites history backwards and all that has been said or done to remove caste-based hierarchies in India:

> See, this country, in its days of greatness, when it was the richest nation on earth, was like a zoo. A clean, well-kept, orderly zoo. Everyone was in his place, everyone happy. Goldsmiths here. Cowherds here. Landlords there. The man called halwai made sweets. The man called a cowherd tended cows. The untouchables cleaned faeces. Landlords were kind to their serfs. Women covered their heads with a veil and turned their eyes to the ground when talking to strange men.

And then, thanks to all those politicians in Delhi, on the fifteenth of August, 1947—the day the British left—the cages had been let open; and the animals had attacked and ripped each other apart and jungle law replaced zoo law. Those that were the most ferocious, the hungriest, had eaten everyone else up and grown big bellies. That was all that was counted now, the size of your belly. It didn't matter whether you were woman, or a Muslim, or an untouchable: anyone with a belly would rise up. My father's father must have been a real Halwai, a sweet-maker, but when he inherited the shop, a member of some other caste must have stolen it from him with the help of the police. My father had not the belly to fight back. That's why he has fallen all the way to the mud, to the level of a rickshaw-puller. That's why I was cheated of my destiny to be fat, and creamy-skinned, and smiling. "To sum up—in the old days there were one thousand castes and destinies in India. These days, there are just two castes: Men with Big Bellies, and Men with Small Bellies. And only two destinies: eat—or get eaten up." (63-64)

While Adiga has adopted a dry, unsentimental, cynical and caustic tone in the novel, he has also successfully portrayed the pictures of the present-day India and given the reader a lot to ponder about. It is as if the author is challenging the reader to contradict him in what he says about India. The focus on the haphazard construction that is going on in the name of development is turning some of India's big metropolis into a jungle of concrete inhabited by people devoid of humaneness; the manner in which "fixers" are found operating for the politicians; the way police forces operate; the dirt, squalor and sub-human conditions in which the poor workers live; are some of the realities that are very difficult to gloss over, let alone ignore by any responsible citizen of India or a discerning reader. Balram calls the poor millions of Indians the "human spiders" (51) as compared to the landlords, the politicians, the middle men and the powerful. If on one hand there are people who move in big air conditioned cars; live in newly built towers with twenty-four hour water and electricity supply; have money to drink the choicest alcohol; visit the glittering malls and shopping arcades; then living by their side and around them are people who drive their cars, build their homes, work for their daily comfort and yet themselves sleep in dormitories, on roads, by the sides of dirty dingy lanes and cook, eat, sleep, defecate and reproduce with no privacy or decent living conditions. The future of the country is in the hands of those who are themselves criminals while the millions who vote in the farce of elections do not get even the basic protection from law or the right to a dignified life for themselves and their children. Speaking about the Great Socialist, Balram tells of how he has used power to fool, exploit and cheat everyone for his personal benefit and his criminal record:

> You see, a total of ninety-three criminal cases—for murder, rape, grand larceny, gun smuggling, pimping and many other such *minor* offences—are pending against the Great Socialist and his ministers at the present moment. Not easy to get convictions when the judges are judging in *Darkness*. (97, my italics)

And Balram is made to sign a confessional statement for an accident that has not happened due to his negligence but only to pre-empt any action against Preeti madam, who in a bout of drunken anger is responsible for the hit and run accident. Thus the binary nature of the Indian reality is again and again brought to the fore by the author so that the reader is forced to take notice of and respond to it. The formless, quiet, unobtrusive people who make life easy and comfortable for the likes of the landlords and the politicians find a legitimate place in *The White Tiger* and offer the reader an insight into what he has always known in the subconscious but chosen to ignore.

An important image that Adiga uses in the novel is that of the white tiger. Right in the beginning of the novel, when the inspector visits the school for a surprise inspection and finds it in a wretched condition with no chairs, no dusters, no uniforms and the students unable to answer simple questions or to read even simple sentences that he writes on the board, it is Balram who stands up to demonstrate his reading and writing skills, which makes the inspector take note of him and proclaim his as "an intelligent, honest, vivacious fellow in this crowd of thugs and idiots." (35) Because of this rare skill of reading and writing shown by Balram, the inspector names him the white tiger. The white tiger is a tiger with a genetic condition that merely eliminates the pigment in the normal orange fur, though it still has dark strips. The white tiger's eyes are very distinct, there being no well defined difference between the yellow of comex and blue of iris. The eyes in some light are practically colourless merely showing the black pupil on a light yellow background. (Wikipedia) True to the name given to him by the school inspector, Balram exhibits a rarity of being that is common to white tigers. The social/moral *pigment* is almost totally absent in Balram, for he will stop at nothing to succeed. During the course of the novel, Balram speaks of the four great poets: "I know by heart the works of the four greatest poets of all time—Rumi, Iqbal, Mirza Ghalib, and a fourth fellow whose name I forget" (6) but surprisingly does not show the sensitivity that the study of the poetry of such great poets would imbue a human being with. At one point in the novel he discusses poetry with a bookseller and shares the verse "*You were looking for the key for years/But the door was always open*" (253). He often sits in the car, in the pose of Buddha while waiting for his master but displays neither the poise nor the justification to his final action of the murder of his master. Though Balram does go through mental rage at his situation and moments of introspection, they are more in the nature of growing resentment and vengefulness towards his situation and the people he works for rather than towards self growth and positive thinking. At one point in the novel, as if like a divine inspiration answers come to Balram,

> *I was looking for the key for years*
> *But the door was always open.* (267)

It is after this that he plans a trip to the national zoo with his nephew Dharam and comes to the enclosure with tall bamboo bars, where a white tiger is housed. "*Not any kind of tiger. The creature that gets born only once every generation in the jungle*" (276). The eye contact that Balram makes with the white tiger is like a moment of epiphany for him and so startling is the revelation that he faints. Later when Dharam writes a letter to his granny, Balram insists that he tell her the whole truth about what happened at the zoo and the letter tells of Balram raving and apologizing again and again for no longer being able to live in a cage:

> They turned to me and said, 'Your uncle is raving—he's saying goodbye to his grandmother. He must think he's going to die.' Uncle's eyes were open now. 'Are you all right, Uncle?' I asked. He took my hand and he said, 'I'm sorry, I'm sorry, I'm sorry.' I asked, 'Sorry for what?' And he said, 'I can't live the rest of my life in a cage, Granny. I'm so sorry.' (278)

By implication it becomes clear that if India is the jungle as Adiga views it, then Balram is the white tiger, who has broken free from the cage. Ironically, the moral dilemma of Balram, in reaching this state of mind is not shared with the reader by Adiga and though the reader can understand the nature of Balram's existence to a great extent and even at some point of time in the novel empathize with his character, he fails to understand or appreciate the choice made by Balram, in changing the circumstance of his life. Balram's claims of his entrepreneur skills and kindness for his employees, towards the end of the novel, appear hollow and boastful and fail to impress the reader. The image of the white tiger is evoked for the final time by Balram to "take the money, and start a school—an English-language school—for poor children in Bangalore. A school where you won't be allowed to corrupt anyone's head with prayers and stories about God or Gandhi—nothing but the facts of life for these kids. A school full of White Tigers, unleashed on Bangalore! We'd have this city at our knees, I tell you. I could become the Boss of Bangalore." (319-20)

Thus *The White Tiger*, brilliant and factual as it is in its depiction of some of the grim realities of the present-day scenario and the malaise that affects the social, political and economic fabric of India, remains at best a breezy, racy reading. Like the 'Murder Weekly' the drivers read in the novel for sensational stories, *The White Tiger* too at times comes close to such type of reading. What saves the novel from falling to a pedestrian level is what appears to be, the honesty of purpose of the author and his desire to shake the reader out of his apathy and warn him that such a revolutionary change might one day come in those who are ignored by the process of historical change. If the multitude of India's population is "half-baked" (10), then its progress also appear to be half baked—carelessly planned and thoughtlessly executed and the reader fails to understand how the future of the world could lie with the "brown man" (5). Of course if the reader were to separate the persona of the author from that of the main character and read everything merely as the perception and categorization of Balram then the book might have a different appeal, but it would reduce the import of what Adiga wishes to convey to the perceptive reader. Therefore whatever be the manner in which the main protagonist speaks to us, and whether or not he offends the reader's sensibility, the book has be viewed as the author's intent to focus on that which has always been relegated to the background or ignored in the past.

Bibliography

Review: http://www.complete-review.com/reviews/india/adigaa.Htm

Truby John, 'Black Comedy', http:/en.wikipedia.org/wiki/Black_ comedy

Adiga Aravind, *The White Tiger*, Harper Collins, New Delhi, 2008.

'The World of Inflation' 'http://www.time.com/time/magazine/article/0,9171,1829868,00.html

'Author Interview' http://www.bookbrowser.com/author_interviews/full/index. cfm?authornumber=1552

Holding the Mirror to the Middle-Class Indian Elite: A Study of *The White Tiger*

AMLANJYOTI PATRA
Infosys, Bhubaneswar

Aravind Adiga's *The White Tiger*, the winner of the Man Booker Prize, 2008, faces adverse criticism: the author is accused of selling an inauthentic picture of Indian poverty to the western market for coming into the limelight. In comparison to *The God of Small things,* it is a simple book, full of wit and black humour, aiming a direct attack at the system of democracy in India. The corrupt politicians and the unholy nexus among the politicians, executives and the business community are ruthlessly exposed, making a poor show of the much advertised 'Shining India'. The present article wants to establish that it is not as much for revealing corruption and poverty as for holding the mirror to the middle-class Indian elite that *The White Tiger* is vehemently criticized.

The satire is direct everywhere in the novel. The protagonist writes to the Chinese Premier who is reported to have made a plan to come to India to witness the progress in technology: "Apparently, sir, you Chinese are far ahead of us in every respect, except that you don't have entrepreneurs. And our nation, though it has no drinking water, electricity, sewage system, public transportation, sense of hygiene, discipline, courtesy, or punctuality, *does* have entrepreneurs. Thousands and thousands of them. Especially in the field of technology. And these entrepreneurs—*we* entrepreneurs—have set up all these outsourcing companies that virtually run America now" (4). Comparing the Indian mass to the roosters, he writes,

> When you get here, you'll be told we Indians invented everything from the Internet to hard-boiled eggs to space-ships before the British stole it all for us.
>
> Nonsense. The greatest thing to come out of this country in the ten thousand years of its history is the Rooster Coop.
>
> Go to Old Delhi, behind the Jama Masjid, and look at the way they keep chickens there in the market. Hundreds of pale hens and brightly coloured roosters, stuffed tightly into wire-mesh cages, packed as tightly as worms in a belly, pecking each other and shitting on each other, jostling just for breathing space; . . . They see the organs of their brothers lying around them. They know they're the next. Yet they do not rebel. They do not try to get out of the coop.
>
> The very same thing is done with human beings in this country. (173-74)

Breaking the myth of the poor but honest Indian people, he writes that the poor people in India appear honest, because they do not have the courage to steal: "It's because 99.9 percent of us are caught in the Rooster Coop just like those poor guys in the poultry market" (175). In page after page, Adiga teases his Indian readers with facts that they carefully keep under the carpet, lest those facts disturb the state of euphoria they are in.

Some facts, however, particularly the fact of corruption in administration, are publicly discussed, thanks to the democratic rule in India that tolerates the freedom of speech. The driver also has the freedom to discuss the corruption in high places: "You see, a total of ninety-three criminal cases—for murder, rape, grand larceny, gun-smuggling, pimping, and many other such minor offences—are pending against the Great Socialist and his ministers at the present moment. Not easy to get convictions when the judges are judging in Darkness, yet three convictions have been delivered, and three of the ministers are currently in jail, but continue to be ministers. The Great Socialist himself is said to have embezzled one billion rupees from the Darkness, and transferred that money into a bank account in a small, beautiful country in Europe full of white people and black money" (97-98). That public discussion of corruption hardly brings any change in the system is ruthlessly exposed through witty comments: "The Great Socialist's enemies seemed to be stronger this election than at the last one. . . . At the tea shop, the gossip grew furious. People sipped their tea and discussed the same things again and again. Would they do it this time? Would they beat the Great Socialist and win the elections? Had they raised enough money of their own, and bribe enough policemen, and brought enough fingerprints of their own, to win? Like eunuchs discussing the *Kama Sutra*, the voters discuss the elections in Laxmangarh" (98).

Adiga's lash of satire is so keen that no one argues with the obvious truth that comes out of the passage quoted above—the booth capturing and all that during election. Rather, the witty and humorous remarks are entertaining. For example, the binary opposition of zoo laws and jungle laws, and that of Big-belly and Small-belly comes from a fantastic voice that "crackles with a kind of joyfully submissive energy":

> See, this country, in its days of greatness, when it was the richest nation on earth, was like a zoo. . . . Everyone in his place, everyone happy. Goldsmiths here. Cowherds here. Landlords there. The man called a Halwai made sweets. The man called a cowherd tended cows. The untouchable cleaned faeces. Landlords were kind to their serfs. . . . And then, thanks to all those politicians in Delhi, on the fifteenth of August, 1947—the day the British left—the cages had been let open; and the animals had attacked and ripped each other apart and jungle law replaced zoo law. Those that were the most ferocious, the hungriest, had eaten everyone else up, and grown big bellies. That was all that counted now, the size of your belly. . . . To sum up—in the old days there were one thousand castes and destinies in India. These days, there are just two castes: Men with Big Bellies, and Men with Small Bellies. And only two destinies: eat—or get eaten up. (63-64)

The readers, the middle-class and the upper middle-class Indians, in particular, enjoy such revelation of reality and at the same time become apprehensive of the protagonist's leg-pulling.

The protagonist, a rickshaw-puller's son turned to a driver who, again, turns out to be an entrepreneur after murdering his master, is in no way a reader-friendly narrator. Rather, he shocks the readers who almost belong to the class of the murdered master, if not to the class of feudal landlords the master's family belongs to. Adiga knows that his readers will take the side of the murdered master Mr. Ashok—the author therefore makes Ashok the target of attack—and will also identify them with him. Like any aspiring middle-class Indian, Ashok studied in America and came back with a Christian wife, one who left him for the States. Unlike his father and brother who continue behaving as feudal lords, Ashok treated the servant class with sympathy and sometimes he also appeared reluctant to bribe the ministers for a smooth running of their family business. Adiga brings out the duplicity in Mr. Ashok only to give his readers a rude shock in a clever way, holding the mirror to their faces. Ashok liked to express his concern for the country whenever he had any opportunity. To his American wife he said, "The thing is, he [the driver] probably has . . . two, three years of schooling in him? He can read and write, but he doesn't get what he's read. He's half-baked. The country is full of people like him, I'll tell you that. And we entrust our glorious parliamentary democracy . . . to characters like these" (10). This is how the educated and well-established Indians usually criticize the function of democracy in India, without any attempt at self-analysis. Adiga mercilessly exposes the facade of such people. Though Ashok repeatedly told his brother Mukesh and his wife Pinky that their driver Balram must be treated as a human being—he even raised his salary without being asked for it—and that he must not be humiliated for his bad English or any other thing, he remained silent when the crime of Pinky was bestowed on Balram. It was Pinky who took the driver's wheel from Balram and killed an urchin on the road during her rash driving. But Balram was made to take the blame—he had to sign a paper prepared by Mukesh that contained his confession of the crime—luckily though, the police did not bother to investigate the death of an urchin and he was saved. This incident of car accident is introduced in the novel as a method of shock-therapy for the readers who easily identify them with Ashok and get terrified to find the protagonist's grudge against the master class people. Again, it was Mr. Ashok who bribed the minister regularly in Delhi so that his family would be exempted of income tax. He knew it very well that this illegal way of getting exempted of income tax is meant for depriving the country of development the expenses of which are met through the taxes collected from the citizens. There seems to be much difference between the theory he uttered and the practice. He rudely caught Balram by the collar calling him names and almost pushed him against the balcony after he learnt that Balram had taken Pinky to the airport. He was not ready to hear anything from Balram and charged him of ruining his family's reputation. "The landlord inside him wasn't dead after all. . . . He pushed me harder against the balcony; my head and chest were over the edge now, and if he pushed me even a bit more I was in real danger of flying over" (182). Any well-to-do man in India is expected to behave in this way in such circumstances.

Ashok is portrayed as a typical middle-class novice—it is not expected from a man of the class he actually belonged to—when he was taken to a foreign prostitute inside a big hotel. "Taking the golden-haired woman with him, the fat man went up to the hotel reception, where the manager greeted him warmly. Mr. Ashok walked behind them and kept looking from side to side, like a guilty little boy about to do something very bad. Half an hour passed. I (Balram) was outside, my hands on the wheel the whole time. I punched the little ogre. I began to gnaw at the wheel. I kept hoping he'd come running out, arms flailing, and screaming, *Balram, I was on the verge of making a mistake! Save me—let's drive away at once!* An hour later Mr. Ashok came out of the hotel—alone, and looking ill" (219). Ashok is portrayed from the perspective of his driver and that too, sympathetically. Here Adiga plays another trick, inducing his readers to get identified with Mr. Ashok who maintains double standards and is sadly lacking in strength of mind that helps one make a choice. Adiga's intention to criticize the middle class mentality is apparent in such descriptions. In one of his short stories, he directly accuses the middle class people of being a part of corruption: "Thousands, sitting around teashops and universities and workplaces every day and every night were cursing corruption. Yet not one fellow had found a way to slay the demon without giving up his share of the loot of corruption" (41). Besides corruption, the middle-class people's narrow-mindedness and petty regional prejudices (as in the remark, "I don't believe a word. The south is full of Tamils. You know who the Tamils are? Negroes. We're the sons of the Aryans who came to India. We made them our slaves. And now they give us lectures") are also exposed in the novel. And thus the book is not an easy read any way. The readers of English novels in India largely come from families that are habituated to take service from servants and who usually have their own vehicles. They don't feel comfortable when they read that the driver Balram has no grudge against the rich Americans who are compelled to do all the odd jobs at home themselves, there being no facility of appointing servants at low price as it is in India. When the politicians are ruthlessly criticized, the middle-class readers find the book entertaining and they are enthusiastic of the author's revelation of the reality. But when they find that the book holds the mirror to their faces, exposing their narrow-mindedness, petty interests, vanity, keenness to save their skins with an apparently indifferent look and their eagerness to pose as a saviour of the underdog, it is intolerable. The best way to express their grudge is to appear as a patriot protesting against the practice of exploiting India's poverty to appease the western readers.

It may be observed in conclusion that whatever Adiga writes in his novel is hard reality presented through satire and black humour. The ever widening gap between the rich and the poor, the rural and the urban, the black spots of child labour and rape that are eating into the very core of Indian society, cannot be denied. The middle-class educated Indian, who has a rather secured life, must be more and more aware of these grim facts and do something constructive to remove all these blemishes. If the effect of globalization is shared by a few and the rest is thrown to the pit of poverty, the country cannot escape tensions between the haves and the have-nots, and it is likely that anytime these tensions may burst up. The only way out of this impasse is not to block the road to globalization, but to spread its effect to all the corners of the society. And the middle-class service-holders are not expected to remain indifferent in this crisis. Instead of competing with the rich through ignoble means, they are expected to be aware of the problems of the poor and take serious steps to remove corruption. Explaining his intention Adiga says, "When India is going through great changes and, with China, is likely to inherit the world from the West, it is important that writers like me try to highlight the brutal injustices of society" (*Times of India,* October 19, 2008). Adiga also hopes that the middleclass Indian will also share his concern for the brutal injustices in the society and do something better than offering lip-service.

Works Cited

Aravind Adiga. *The White Tiger* (New Delhi: Harper Collins, 2008).

_____. *Between the Assassinations* (Picador, 2008).